AF560612

DPH Education Series

NON-FORMAL AND CONTINUING EDUCATION

U K SINGH • K N SUDARSHAN

DISCOVERY PUBLISHING HOUSE
NEW DELHI-110002

First Published – 2001

Reprinted – 2017

ISBN: 978-81-7141-371-3

Non-formal and Continuing Education

Published by:

DISCOVERY PUBLISHING HOUSE PVT. LTD.

4383/4B, Ansari Road Darya Ganj
New Delhi - 110 002 (India)
Phone: +91-11-23279245, 43596064-65
Fax: +91-11-23253475
E-mail: discoverypublishinghouse@gmail.com
sales@discoverypublishinggroup.com
web: www.discoverypublishinggroup.com

Printed at:
Infinity Imaging Systems
Delhi

Preface

The *DPH Education Handbook* has been created to provide access to information about contemporary topics in education. Practitioners and students at all levels in education have a need to know what is happening today, in addition to historical treatments within the literature.

Each chapter within the Handbook is designed to provide the user with needed "state-of-the-art" information as well as further sources of information. One of the significant features of each chapter is the inclusion of specific programmes, projects and activities so that the researcher can locate human resources as well as the literature.

The handbook will be of use to graduate and post graduate students in education and to practicing teachers, administrators, librarians and planners. The chapters and the further sources of information cited in each book should lead the reader to thousands of people and documents for either research or programme planning purposes.

An effort to achieve universal and effective education is based on a recognition of the rights of students to basic education that enables them to thrive in a complex society, as well as a realization the technological and economic growth is facilitated by increasing the numbers of students, even those with poor academic progresses, who are, in fact successful in learning. Thus, recent and current efforts improve education serve both private and social interests.

This series is addressed to administrators, planners and educators working in the field of education and training with a view to stimulating interest and attention in the areas of education and its related fields. It is also addressed to a growing number of teachers and instructors who will be practitioners in education and who will need to be acquainted with the modern aspects of educational practice and development. Many ideas, generalisations and discussions presented in this series should also prove useful to employing organisations committed to provide training facilities within their establishments—leading to effective mutual participation by institutions and organisations.

The editors wishes to thank the contributors, as well as those organizations that gave permission to publish their extracts, chapters etc.

Editors

Contents

1

Non-Formal Education

When the project was designed, it was fully realised that the field programme staff would have a pioneering role to play in this experimental study. Their academic qualifications, experience in life, maturity of mind, familiarity with the local language, their tact and ability to deal with any situation that might suddenly come up, would go a long way towards contributing to the success or failure of the experiment. These considerations were kept in mind while recruiting them.

Recruitment procedures

In order to recruit the action programme staff, information about these vacancies, nature of their work, salary and other conditions of service were sent to Nurses' Training Schools. Teachers' Training Schools, Employment Exchange and the concerned offices at the district level. The aim was to recruit candidates from the Telengana area as the language spoken there was different from the coastal area Telugu. The qualifications laid down for these positions and the number required were:

Designation	formal qualifications	Number required	
		Phase 1	Phase II
Maternity Assistant	Certificate in General Nursing	2	6
Health Educator	Auxiliary Nurse Midwife Certificate	4	12
Functional Literary Supervisor	Secondary School Leaving Certificate, and Secondary Grade Basic Training Certificate	1	2
Functional Literacy Teacher	Elementary Grade Basic Training Certificate	2	4

Of the personnel recruited on the basis of qualifications mentioned above, twelve field workers had no previous experience in teaching while eight has some experience. With exception of two of the Literacy Teachers, all the others were in the age-group of 20-25-perhaps too young to be effective Non-formal Educators or rural women, most of whom were older and more experienced in life. Further, only ten workers were married.

Training schedules

For organising the training programme it was decided that about two thirds of the total training time of six weeks should be used for pre-service training and the remainder for in-service training courses of short duration. A draft syllabus was drawn up for a pre-service training of about four weeks duration and was divided into four main sections: (1) background and orientation to the project; (2) subject matter content; (3) implementation of programme in the field including practical work in teaching methods, use of audio-visual aids, medical check-up; and (4) role of field staff in assisting research and evaluation

The training course for staff in Phase 1 was conducted from 4 to 21 June 1973 at Hyderabad and from 22 to 29 June 1973 at Mahbubnagar and in the villages selected for Phase 1. The training course of staff in Phase II was conducted from 17 September to 4 October 1973 at Mahbubnagar as the action programme in Phase II was to begin in the first week of October 1973. The medium of begin.

As the participants came in, most of them with one or two young children with them, they were seated in a U-shaped manner. The Health Educator sat at the open end, with the black-board, charts, etc., needed for the evening on the wall, behind her. The village women were not very time-conscious, and so the Health Educator usually allowed a few minutes, after the scheduled starting time, for the latecomers to join. Then she took the roll-call and the attendance was recorded in a specially designed register.

Starting with the photograph

To start a discussion on a problem/topic in the curriculum, the appropriate photograph or other illustration depicting the problem or directly connected with the problem was first shown to the group. Then the Health Educator posed some questions to lead the participants into a discussion of the problem. By using questions suggested in the Discussion Guide, the discussion was conducted by her and through this method, the message or messages were transmitted to the participants. The appropriate visual materials indicated in the Weekly Lesson Guide were also used and the group was asked to consider solutions to the problem and the action to be taken by them. In the case of some problems or topics, where live demonstrations were necessary, the Health Educator, usually with the guidance ad help of the Maternity Assistant, arranged for such demonstrations. Towards the end of the class-time, the Health Educator gave a summary of the day's lesson, stressing the main messages of the lesson and action to be taken.

'Known to the Unknown': Thus, the method used was based on the educational principle of 'known to unknown' through guided group discussion. At the conclusion of the day's lesson, roll-call was again taken and recorded to mark those who had come in after the first roll call. The basic maternity services and distribution of medicines and supplementary food was done after the class was over and such services were given only to those who attended the class.

When the group met the next day, the Health Educator would begin the class with a recapitulation of the previous day's lesson and the messages it conveyed and would clear the doubts, if any. Then she went on to introduce the day's lesson as described above. Each class was visited by the Project Officer at least twice a week for supervision, guidance on group discussion and any further explanation of subject-matter.

Need for even progress among centres

In the first five months of Phase 1, the Health Educators were allowed some flexibility with regard to the time necessary for covering a problem/topic, but it was found that the rate of progress was uneven and varied considerably form center to centre. Therefore, in December 1973, the centres lagging behind were given about two weeks to catch up with the others; the latter were asked to review the previous lessons and not to proceed with new lessons. This was done in order to bring all classes to the same stage in the curriculum, so that Weekly Lesson Guides could be introduced from then on.

From the middle of December 1973, Weekly Lesson Guides prepared by the Project Officer were distributed to each centre and the Health Educators were asked to try to cover each day's lesson as indicated in Weekly Lesson Guide. This procedure has been of great help to the Health Educators in covering the problems/topics in the syllabus. The last two weeks were utilised by them for review of the entire of non-formal education in MCCs.

Learning through discussion

The women participants had never been to a school or participated in any educational activity earlier. So, they needed a little tome to adjust themselves to this programme based on discussion as a method of learning. The Health Educators conducted also some practice lessons in the beginning of Phase II, from 29 April to 18 May, 1974. By that time, conditions had stabilised and the regular classes as per course content were started. The unitised lessons covering the subject areas, the relating to Maternal Health Care commenced on 20 May 1974.

A set of twenty-two lessons covering the subject were given in the centres during the period from 20 May to 8 July, 1974. In view of the special importance of this subject area to rural mothers, twelve revision lessons on this chapter were programmed during the period 12 to 30 July, 1974. The impact of these lessons on the participants in six MCC and six MCC+FLIT Centres was assessed by the Project Officer during September 1974. Of the 70 participants who were examined, 35 secured 35 per cent or more.

The course content

A set of thirteen lessons relating to the subject area of Child Development and Rearing Practices was covered from 1 to 16 November, 1974. This was followed by a set of twenty lessons relating to the subject area of Health Care of Infants ad Toddlers. They were programmed during the period from 20 November to 12 December, 1974. A set of four lessons covering the subject area of responsibility parenthood was programmed during 13 and 18 December, 1974.

These were followed by the lessons relating to the last subject area in the course content, viz., General Knowledge. It covered information on available services, agriculture, crops of the district, growing of vegetables, poultry, responsibilities of a citizen, and democracy. These lessons, twenty-eight in number, were covered between 20 December 1974 and 7 February 1975.

Having completed the course content at a reasonable pace, it was felt tat a set of nine revision lessons covering the total course content and an internal assessment were desirable. Though, they were programmed between 8 and 19 February, 1975, only four of the revision lessons could be covered, as the classes and activities in all the centres were stopped on 15 February 1975. However, the internal assessment was completed by the Project Officer in all the six MCC and six MCC+FLIT centres between 12 and 28 February, 1975. The results obtained and the analysis of the answers given by the 141 participants were useful in the revision of materials. Ninety one members out of the 141 participants examined secured 12 points or more out of a maximum of 30 points.

The problem of chronic absenteeism

Some of the problems faced in implementing the programme of Nonformal Education in Phase II are presented here. The major ailment suffered by the programme was chronic absenteeism on the part of the participants.

Effective environment: The number of participants enrolled and the number of absentees resulting in a considerably reduced effective enrolment is given in the table.

The magnitude of chronic absenteeism in MCC and MCC +FLIT centres was quite high and required some consideration. It was indeed strange that the attendance could be so low even when incentives in the form of medical care and supplementary feeding were provided. The problem required scrutiny and solution. Therefore, an examination of the educational status of the husbands of the participants was attempted and the information is presented in the table.

Effect of home environment: It will be observed from table II that the husbands of only 94 participants out of the 317, i.e., 29.6 per cent enrolled in the twelve centres wee literate. Twenty-two out of the 94 such participants, i.e., 23.4 per cent of those with a literacy environment at home were among the chronic absentees. Similarly 223 participants out of the 317 participants, i.e., 70.4 per cent enrolled in all the twelve centres had an illiteracy environment at home. Seventy eight out of those 223, i.e., 35.0 per cent wee among the chronic absentees. These data indicate that the literacy or illiteracy environment at home plays a considerable role in chronic absenteeism of an illiterate woman enrolled for an educational programme. The chance for absenteeism may be considered to be enhanced nearly by one and half times by an illiterate environment at home.

Reasons for absenteeism: Average monthly attendance for 10 months is given in table Ii. In an educational programme, attendance and regularity of the participants is an index of the response to the programme and the success achieved by it. The following factors markedly influenced the attendance of the participants in the Non-formal Education class.

— The imperative need for earning 'daily wages' for making a living is a common problem faced by the rural women. They have to seek work wherever it is available, and they can never be sure of finding work in their own village all through the year. So they have to migrate to nearby or far-off places in search of work. This migration inevitably reduces their effective participation in an experiment. Paying a visit to the mother's place is a common tendency among village women. In the case of young mothers, it is more frequent. Festivals and Jataras are also responsible for the movement of the rural folk from place. Short visits originally planned often turn out to be long ones of considerable duration.

— The selected sample consists of two currently pregnant women as participants in each of the villages. Some confinement could naturally be expected as a common feature in every centre. Absence on account of the arrival of the new child varies from 3 to 8 weeks.

— Besides these factors, rain, darkness, courtesy visits of relatives, occurrences like death, birth, marriage, local entertainment, accidents in the village, quarrels among the participants, scare created by quarrelsome husbands who would not tolerate any delay in the return of their wives form the Centre, were some of the other reasons influencing the day's attendance.

A total of 158 participants in each of the MCC and MCC+FLIT centres were enrolled in Phase II programme. The factors enumerated above affected the sample and among the participants there were chronic absentees. The attendance of the number of participants month by month from May 1974 onwards till February 1975 reveals that 69 out of 106 participants or 65 per cent were present on an average during any month in the MCC centres while 83 out of 111 participants or 74.8 per cent took advantage of the programme in the MCC + Flit centres.

Departmental and staff difficulties

It was also noticed that during the first five months of the programme, i.e., May 1974 to September 1974 the participation steadily increased in both the MCC and MCC+FLIT centres. The attendance during those months touched the maximum of 80.2 per cent tin the case of the MCC centres and 88.3 per cent in the case of the MCC + FLIT centres. This period also synchronised with the period when work for the agriculture-labour participation would generally be available in the villages. This period was followed by a period of decline in attendance touching the minimal in class attendance during the phase, viz., 55.7 per cent in the case of MCC villages and 58.6 per cent in the case of MCC + FLIT centres. The villages and 58,6 per cent in the case of MCC + FLIT centres.

Departmental and staff difficulties

It was also noticed that during the first five months of the programme, i.e., May 1974 to September 1974 the participation steadily increased in both the MCC and MCC + FLIT centres. The attendance during those months touched the maximum of 80.2 per cent tin the case of the MCC centres and 88.3 per cent in the case of the MCC + FLIT centres. This period also synchronised with the period when work for the agriculture-labour participation would generally be available in the villages. This period was followed by a period of decline in attendance touching the minimal in class attendance during the phase, viz., 55.7 per cent in the case of MCC villages and 58.6 per cent in the case of MCC + FLIT centres. The decline in attendance during the period that followed October 1974 was also probably caused to some extent by: (i) lack of the Salad oil for distribution during October 1974, (ii) absence of glamour for the programme which by that time had become quite familiar, and (iii) migration of participants seeking work elsewhere.

The young women workers were also exposed to problems of different kinds. These were: infection and periodic illness caused by insanitary conditions, emotional stresses and strains, inter-staff relationship, and lack of teaching aids.

Effective enrolment by centres

Name of the Centre	Enrolment	Chronic absentees	Effective enrolment
A. MCC treatment			
Maddigatla	25	14	11
Elkicherla	30	11	21
Md. Hussainpalle	28	6	23
Nizalpur	27	3	24
Bandarpalle	30	12	18

Gurakonda	19	7	12
Sub-Total	159	53	109
B. MCC + FLIT Treatment			
Kotha Molgara	30	7	23
Patha Molgara	26	13	13
Polkampalle	24	5	19
Tadikonda	24	8	16
Parpalle	26	9	17
K. Malkapur	28	5	23
Sub-Total	158	47	111
Total	317	100	220

Table II. Educational status of husbands of participants by centres (Phase II)

Name of the Centre	No. of par ticipants whose hus bands are literate	Chronic absentees among them	No. of par ticipants whose hus bands are illiterate	Chronic absentees among them
A. MCC Treatment				
Maddigatla	8	5	17	9
Elkicherla	5	5	25	6
Md. Hussainpalle	5	-	23	6
Nizalpur	11	1	16	2
Gurakonda	8	2	11	5
Sub Total	49	16	110	37
B. MCC + FLIT Treatment				
Kotha Molgara	13	1	17	6
Patha Molgara	4	-	22	13
Polkampalle	4	-	20	5
Tadikonda	1	-	23	8
Parpalle	11	4	15	5
K. Mlakapur	12	1	16	4
Sub Total	45	6	113	41
Total	94	22	223	78

2

Complementarity Between Formal and Non-formal Education

Complementarity which means to bring about mutual support between the two channel of formal and non-formal education in respect of personnel, facilities and administrative structures, is essential for the effective implementation of the programme of universalization of elementary education. Complementarity also shares the curriculum, instructional materials, methods of teaching, evaluation/certification procedures and techniques etc, it may be planned or vicarious and may also occur as a result of efforts to coordinate educational programme at the local, block, sub-district, district, state or national levels. It has further assumed significance in view of the NEP which stresses the compatibility of educational standards in formal and non-formal education.

The concept of complementarity between formal and non-formal education is reflected in the national Policy of education. Article 45 of Indian Constitution enjoins upon the provision of free, compulsory and universal education upto the age of 14 years. Both the systems are attempting to fulfil the constitutional obligation of universal elementary education. The New Education Policy has also recommended to coordinate the network of non-formal education fully for realising the target of universal education by 1990 upto the age of 11 years and by 1995 upto the age of 14 years. The responsibility for implementing the above obligation rests with the Ministry of Human Resources development. It, however, also seeks support from other Ministries. Complementarity lies with the objectives of formal and non-formal education. Both the system of formal and non-formal education aim at improving the quality of life and raising the living standards. The major objectives of the system is to develop the personality of the child through inculcating values, attitudes and other necessary skills of life so that the children can become productive members of the society. They can become good citizens and can serve the society and nation in a better way.

Conceptually, there is complementarity between both the system in terms of achieving the objectives of human resources development. Non-formal education has been introduced to cater the needs of out-of-school children who are either drop-out from formal schools at various stages or have never been to school who could not avail of the facilities provided by the formal system due to socio-economic compulsions. It also intends to meet the essential learning needs of children living in remote and sparsely populated areas where the establishment of the formal school is considered to be non-viable. The character of flexibility brings complementarity in both the systems. Non-formal education has character of flexibility in respect of timings, vacations, curriculum and multiple point entry, etc. and adjustment according to local specific needs of the area and locality. The formal set up is also following the character of flexibility and encouraging multiple point entry. School hours, school vacations and curriculum are adjusted according to needs of the community. However, the practices vary from state to state. The Delhi School Education Act 1973, specifically permits multiple point entry of students. It has been observed that such a provision is generally used for the purpose of allowing transfer of students from one formal school to another at different stages of education. The state of Uttar Pradesh has positive attitude towards formal and non-formal education. The students from non-formal education centres are allowed to appear at class V examination with the students of formal schools and are allowed to join class VI in formal schools after qualifying the examination.

Human resources are also shared in both the systems of formal and non-formal education. Clientele in the non-formal education are either drop-outs or non-attending children. The students who are drop-outs are from formal schooling. In most of the states teachers are also from the formal schools who teach in non-formal education centres. They are getting additional payment for working in these centres. Regarding the training of the teachers, services of the same teacher educators, lecturers, principals and resources persons are utilized in training the teachers from the State Institute of Education, Universities, Training Colleges and Resources Centres in both the systems. Regarding supervision and inspection, mostly same supervisory staff of the formal set up is deployed for these NFE centres. District Education Officers (DEO) and District Inspectors of school (DIS) supervise and inspect these NFE centres also from time to time. At the Directorate level, in some states services of the same Director of Public Instruction (DPI) has been utilized for looking after the work of both the formal and non-formal education.

Curriculum also plays vital role in establishing the complementarity between formal and non-formal education because the standard in any of the system can't be lower than that of the other. It is emphasised in New Education Policy that all necessary measures will be taken to ensure that the quality of non-formal education is comparable with formal education. No doubt, the curriculum is based on the demand and need of the people as it is local specific and problem based. Relevance, practicability and flexibility are the main criterion for the NFE curriculum. Health, vocation, environment, social awareness literacy and numeracy are the dimensions of the NFE curriculum. These criterion is must for NFE but it may be followed in the formal set up also. The aim of both the curricula is to enable the child to acquire certain competencies, skills and knowledge at the primary and middle stages. Besides this the content of education in formal and non-formal sectors has been generally centered around certain learning outcomes expected to be attained by the learners at the end of primary/elementary stage. The attainment of learners are evaluated on the basis of the learning outcomes specified in the Minimum Learning Continuum (MLC) developed by the NCERT. It has also attempted that the content should be derived from the real situations in both formal and non-formal education. In addition to this, a common machinery is being prepared the instructional materials and curriculum for formal and non-formal education. The NCERT is preparing the curriculum and instructional material at the national level and SIE, SISE, SCERT, SIERT and SRC are preparing the curriculum at the state level. In most of the state M.P. Model condensed version of formal curriculum is being utilised in the non-formal education.

The methodology used in the NFE is different from formal education and different pedagogical strategies have been utilised to cater the needs of the children in both the systems. The teachers in NFE centres are generally deployed from the formal set up and they teach in both the system according to the needs and situation of the students. In both the system the teacher rearrange the content according to the needs of students and is also free to use available resources in teaching. Teacher helps the children in preparing teaching aids like charts, album, drawing cards, free hand sketching, wood toys and clay toys etc. in both the systems according to their situations. Media is common strategy in both the system. Dialogue, role playing, simulation, group discussion and problem solving are the teaching methods commonly used in both formal and non-formal education. The theoretical and practical knowledge of vocational skills is also provided effectively in non-formal centres through socially useful productive work (SUPW) because the children in the centres are coming from such homes, where they are already busy with such activities like agriculture, fisheries bamboo and woodwork etc. Except this, like formal school curriculum and co-curricular activities are also organised in NFE centres. National festivals, like Independence day and Republic Day etc. are celebrated with the help of the community participation and involvement.

Mass-media is one of the important means to integrate formal and non-formal education. The educational programmes of both the systems are fruitfully broadcasted by INSAT 1-B which is already in operation in the country. Twenty either stations of the All India Radio (AIR) have already been linked with the INSAT based radio net work. Special equipment has been installed at these stations to receive programmes directly from the satellite. The programmes of education both in schools and NFE centres will be imparted through Radio as well as TV network meaningfully. Another UNICEF aided project on mass-media is being implemented by the NCERT in collaborations with the state governments. The educational media-Radio, Television and low cost teaching aids is helping in reaching the children hitherto unreached and also improving the quality of education impared through both the systems of education.

The UNICEF-assisted projects in education sectors are being implemented to provide relevant curriculum and methodology for both the systems to promote the universalisation of elementary education by NCERT in collaboration with state education departments. The projects include Early Childhood Education (ECE), primary Education Curriculum Renewal (PECR), Comprehensive Access to primary Education (CAPE), Nutrition, Health, Education and Environmental Senitation (NHEES), Development Activities in Community Education and Participation (DACEP), etc. Through these projects new contents and methods using environment oriented and problem solving approaches are being developed for both formal and non-formal education.

Another area of complementarity refers to the linkages between formal and non-formal education. Basic skill training consists of literacy, numeracy and technology in other words communication, life and productive skill is being imparted to both the system of formal and non-formal education. According to the recommendations of national Council for Teacher Education (NCTE), most of the states have modified the primary teacher education curriculum to prepare would-be-teachers for both the system through the same process. Under the UNICEF-assisted project Comprehensive Access to Primary Education (CAPE) of NCERT, the learning material for the out of schools children is being prepared following the approach training-cum-production and this approach has been introduced in the curriculum of teacher training institutes in different states. The teacher trainee has to prepare relevance-based learning materials, i.e. capsule and module. In some of the states non-formal education centres are attached to the primary teacher training institute for orienting the trainees about the functioning of non-formal education. In addition to this, non-formal education has been envisioned in pre-service training. Teachers from formal set up are being provided training about the functioning of non-formal education through in-service training and short-term course organised by the State Institute of Education, (SIE), State Institute of Science Education (SISE), State Council of Educational Research and Training (SCERT), State Institute of Educational Research and Training (SIERT) and State Resources Centres (SRC) etc.. The erstwhile Centre of Education Technology (CET) now called Central Institute of Educational Technology (CIET), a constituent of NCERT, under the project 'Satellite Instructional Television Experiment (SITE) provided training to 4,8000 primary school teachers in one year in both content of science and approach of science teaching. Such programmes support both the systems.

Complementarity lies in administration and

organisation of both the systems of education from top to bottom level. The Bureau of School Education of Ministry of Human Resources Development (MHRD) is administering both the type of education at the national level. NCERT as an academic wing of MHRD coordinate academic activities of both the systems and prepare curriculum and methodology according to needs and problems. The administrative set up for formal and non-formal education, however, differs from state to state. Three types of administrative models are functioning at the state level. In some states formal and non-formal education are administered by the Directorate of Adult Education and still in some others formal, non-formal and adult education come within preview of one single Directorate of Education. At the district level in the States, District Education Officers and District inspector of Schools are practically looking after the work of supervision and inspection of non-formal education. In these states, where non-formal education has been tagged with adult education, the administration, supervision and inspection are looked after by the District Adult Education Officers. Block Education Officers and Extension Education Officers are responsible for looking after the job of supervision and inspection of both the system at block level. Village Education Committee and parent Teacher Association are responsible for the management, supervision and inspection of both the system at village level. School complex is also an important means to strengthen integrated functioning of schools and non-formal education centres. In each complex there is a central school which is generally a high/higher secondary school in which about ten to twelve primary schools and about five to seven middle schools within the radius of five to seven kilometers participated within a month or fortnightly. All sorts of difficulties regarding administration, management, curriculum, methodology and other problems of implementation of various programmes in both formal and non-formal education are discussed in the complex meetings and all possible help is provided by the central school to solve their problems. Such complex strengthen Complementarity between both the system.

Facilities and resources are also shared in both the set-ups. NCERT, Universities, Teacher Training Institutions, SIE, SCERT and SRC etc. are used by both the systems for academic guidance and consultations services, seminars, short-term courses, conferences, and training courses are organised in the above institutions for both formal and non-formal education. Most of the NFE centres are also running in the school buildings in the evenings though at some places these are running in temples, churches, mosques, community centres and dharamshala etc. Besides this surveys are conducted in respect of boys and girls for organising the NFE centres and reports are maintained. Attendance registers are maintained for checking the regularity of the students. Stock registers, teacher diaries are also kept for judging the progress of the children.

Non-formal education is also financed by the Ministry of Human Resources Development like formal education. The MHRD provides grants to nine educationally backward states on the basis of 50:50, 90:10 in case of exclusively for girls and hundred per cent in case of voluntary organisation for running these NFE centres. Teacher's salaries, student remuneration, and contingent grants are paid out of these grants. Though the teachers are paid much less as compared to the formal school teachers but this is effective way of utilising the limited resources of the nation for meeting the ever increasing demands of the people.

Lastly evaluation of both the systems enforces complementarity. Children though in NFE system are not only evaluated in terms of performance in examination like formal system but in terms of personality development like social, emotional and mental, etc... The children are compared and evaluated with themselves viz, with their previous achievement at different levels. The record of previous reports are kept for judging the rate of development. Besides this children are given facilities to appear in the main examination or at supplementary examination or both according to his own-conveniences after completing all the prescribed courses/units/syllabus at the V and VIII standard examination conducted by the District and the Divisional Boards respectively.

The preceding discussion reveals the complementarity between the formal and non-formal education. The complementarity was presented in terms of objectives, curriculum, methodology, administration, finance and evaluation and for promoting and achieving the goal universalisation of elementary education, at desired level. It is hoped that the complementarity linkages and coordinated planning and implementation envisaged in the New Education Policy will make it more effective.

3

Innovative Programs: Formal and Non-Formal Education

The endemic problem of adult illiterates coupled with the poor performance of primary education has plagued the education development and is creating socio-economic inequities in Pakistan. The efforts to promote primary education were considered necessary in the country soon after its inception on the map of the world in 1947. The problem of adult illiterates was not given enough attention with the result that country has 53.40 million adult illiterates in 1990. the literacy ratio is 30% sharp differences between male and female and rural and urban population. The literacy for urban males is 55.3% but it is as low as 1.7% for rural females in one of the provinces. Similarly only 63.5% of the primary school are group children have access to schools and 50 of those drop out before completing the five year cycle. Several policy documents and five year development plans set targets to achieve universal primary education and increase literacy ratio to 90%. But the target dates were reset in every policy and plan. The reasons for this poor performance in basic education are varied and complex. Several strategies and programes were tried to achieve UPE and promote literacy but most of the programmes were based on adhoc planning and poor implementation. As a result the success rate was modest and several programes were abandoned half way and wasted lot of scarce financial resources. For these experiences it became evident that formal education programes have failed to meet the demands of basic education. Curriculum was rigid and irrelevant to the needs of rural masses and kept a huge population away from the formal education institutions.

This case study is an attempt to analyze different formal and non-formal education programes in the sectors of primary education and literacy. However, the specific objectives of this study are as follows:

- Why Pakistan has lagged behind so much in promoting literacy rate?
- Why the different innovative programes have serious implementation deficiencies?
- Why the targets of universal primary education have been elusive?
- What can be learnt from different programmes of primary education?

Following four programmes will be discussed and analyzed to draw conclusions and strategies for future planning and implementation:

- Experimental Pilot Project Integrating Education and Rural Development (EPPIERD) 1977/Rural Education and Development (READ) 1980;
- Primary Education Project (PEP) 1979-1984;
- Nai Roshni Schools 1987-88;
- IQRA Pilot Project 186-87.

The READ and IQRA Pilot Projects adopted non-formal education strategies to promote literacy. The READ Project though experimental in nature and only extended to Federal area of Islamabad was based on different programmes whereas the IQRA Project imparted only literacy skills of reading and writing.

The PEP and Nai Roshni Schools were the projects for primary education under formal school system. PEP was a pilot project to experiment the utility of some inputs to increase enrollment, decrease drop out, improve the quality of education and make primary education cost effective. The Nai Roshni provided a second chance to primary school drop outs or to those who could not attend to primary schools because of any reason between the age of 5 to 9 years.

These four programes/project have been selected because they provide a range of information to over formal as well as non-formal education and also analyze literacy versus primary education programes.

Analysis of innovative educational projects:

A) Experimental Pilot Project Integrating Education and Rural Development (EPPIERD) 1977/Rural Education and Development (READ) 1980

This project was started in 1977 in collaboration with UNESCO having following objectives for a period of five years:

Objectives

i) Endeavour to develop and test models of primary education which may be made available to the maximum number of rural children. These models would involve feasible structures, curricula, methods, textbooks, teaching aids and materials.

ii) Attempt to establish improved educational services to be extended to an increasing number of primary school leavers and other who need sound basic pre-vocational education and/or training.

iii) Develop and test new skill-oriented programes for children, youths and adults, in fields such as literacy and numeracy, general education, civics, crop and animal husbandry, agro-technical subjects, arts and crafts, cottage industries, health, nutrition, home improvement and population education

iv) Develop new communication and learning techniques including radio, community audio media, education by correspondence, games, team and peer teaching and relating the program to the milieu, using the suitable combinations of mean and channels.

v) Assist in the training and/or retraining of educational personnel to provide necessary orientation or reorientation to the community and its environment and potential.

The project was designed as a part of a larger effort by the government of Pakistan to integrate educational programes with rural development and promote better economic opportunities for rural development. The project only made a modest beginning during the first four years hence it was modified in 1980-81 and renamed as Rural Education and Development.

Strategy

The project was launched in 32 villages. In any such program of rural development, with an overwhelming component of education, suffers from lack of motivation of people for whom the project was launched. In view of this difficulty the village people were made fully aware of the objectives of the project, how it was to be implemented and what expected results were to be achieved. The project management was ensured following activities:

- Organize Village Education Committees in order to have organized planning and management bodies for rural development.
- Held a seminar for headmasters/headmistresses to acquaint them with the methodology and procedure of administering the questionnaires for pre-launching survey.
- Conducted village surveys with the help of the headmasters/headmistresses and members of the Village Education Committees.
- Analyzed the raw data in order to have an overall view of the needs, problems resources, and dynamics of power of each of the project villages.
- Periodic but regular visits of the project staff to the project areas for rapport and monitoring.

A mix of strategies of normal and non-formal approaches were adopted to accommodate flexibility in the implementation of the programme. an integrated package of different components was based on following strategies:

- Purely non-formal education activities of universalization of primary education.
- Integrated formal and non-formal education programmes to increase the effectiveness of elementary school education through combination of basic skills consistent with the occupational needs of the community.

- Formal education with improved curricula, textbooks, instructional materials and teaching/learning aids through massive use of instructional technology.
- Integrated package of non-formal education components to provide economic motivation, socio-cultural development and educational services to community.

Inputs/outputs

On the basis of needs of rural people the project activities/ inputs were designed for children, youth and adults to enable them to participate in the socio-economic development of the village. A package of five components was developed for the project (i) village workshops, (ii) women education centre, communing viewing centres, (iii) adult literacy centres, (iv) Mohallah schools, and (v) Mosque schools. A brief description of each component is presented:

Village Workshops: The village workshop was to provide skill training to village youth and untrained manpower. A skilled *mistry* was appointed at a fixed salary of Rs.500/- per month to conduct the training of participants on these trades i.e. wood work, masonry and metal work. Each workshop was provided necessary tools and some consumable material. The workshops were expected to generate funds from the sale of their products. Twenty five workshops were established from 1980 to 1984.

Fifteen of these workshops provided training in wood work, four in metal work and two in masonry. Four workshops were closed for different reasons. About 194 students were enrolled in twenty one workshops and average enrollment per workshop was 9 trainees. The record of these workshops revealed that about 12 workshops were able to sell articles produced by the trainees at a cost of Rs.23,864/- during four year period. The average sale proceeds of the workshop was Rs.1988/- which was more than the amount of any other such project/experience. About 26 students were trained during this period from village workshops.

The trainees who had spent 5 to 6 months in the workshops did not progress in the skill development to such an extent that they could be self employed. The major reason was that instructors/craftsmen were not trained to teach skills. The craftsmen were food in their skills but teaching was a difficult part. Secondly the students did not attend the workshops regularly because of different local problems. The raw material was not provided in adequate supply and it could not be replenished either. The experience had a limited success but could prove useful if the project was modified, instructors were trained in pedagogy, more raw material provided, modern trades such as welding, electricity were introduced, only interested committed students to be enrolled and above all the level of skills should be attained to such an extent that after the completion of training the trainee could start work/earn money at his own.

Women Education Centers/Community Viewing Centers: These centers were established for out of school girls and under-employed rural women to provide training in the income generating skills like sewing, knitting, embroidery and poultry farming. A locally qualified and experienced female teacher was appointed at the centre with a fixed salary Rs.300/- p.m. In accordance with the requirement of each centre one sewing and one knitting machine were provided. Thirty two centres were established to provide skill training to the students for income generation. This earning could raise the standard of living or respective families. The total enrollment was 773 in 32 centres with an average of 24 trainees per centre. The drop out rate of trainees was 30% from these centres and the major reasons were: (i) marriage outside the village; (ii) lack of job opportunities after training (iii) poverty of the trainers and unable to purchase raw material (iv) household chores. The standard of material produced by the trainees was satisfactory. The income generating objective of centres was not achieved because the trained graduates of these centres were not producing for the market but the products were made for family needs and friends. In this way it was difficult to assess the financial contribution made to the family. Another important objective was to bring desired change in the attitude of rural population which was imperative that new skills should be introduced and encouraged and also the traditional skills may be modified according to local needs. It was considered necessary to provide a bulk supply of raw material on reasonable price to these centres. It was also found out that the training of teachers/instructors was necessary to make these centres work efficiently. The community viewing centres also provided literacy skills to females. Each teacher/resource person was given Rs.150/- per month for teaching literacy. These centres provided a good combination of income generating and literacy skills.

Adult Literacy Centers: The illiteracy problem is serious in Pakistan with only 16.1% literacy rate for females according to the 1981 census. The extreme cases in rural areas are grim where female literacy is as low as 1.7%. The project established 17 centers out of which 13 were for males and 4 for females. The enrollment of adult illiterate was 184 students hence the average enrollment per centre was 12 students.

The adult literacy centres were opened for both male and female to make rural masses literate. One instructor for each centre was appointed to impart the skills reading, writing and numeracy. The performance of literacy centres was very good and most of adults who joined the centres were made literate although relapse into illiteracy was common.

Mohallah Schools: Under the READ Project Mohallah Schools were opened in those villages where there were no facilities for primary education or the school was not within the walking distance of children. Those schools imparted education to girls of different age groups. The accommodation for the school was provided by the Village Education Committee. The teacher was paid an honorarium of Rs.150/- per month. By 1984 about 26 Mohallah schools were established in project area but 5 had to close down because of different reasons. The total enrolment was 1258 in the remaining 23 schools with an average of 55 students per school. The percentage of enrolled students was the highest in pre-class I & II which was 58%. The lack of teachers posed a serious problem to the successful functioning of the Mohallah Schools. Each if the teachers became available they were not competent to teach. The casual behavior and irregularity of students was not conducive to the successful functioning of Mohallah schools.

Mosque Schools: The problem of access for primary school age children is a serious issue. It is not only the lack of schools but the inability of the students to reach school is also a constraint. The rising cost of building primary schools could be reduced if the mosque could be used as school after Fajar prayers. The mosque is available in each settlement or vicinity in Pakistan which reduces physical distance and enable the children to attend schools. In the project area thirty seven mosque schools were opened. Each school was provided black board and teaching material. The teaching was done by Imam of the mosque who got honorarium of Rs. 150/- per month and a teacher who got the salary of Rs.300/- per month. The component of mosque school was most successful in the project. It provided easy access to school, increased enrolment and reduced cost because the cost on building was altogether saved. The curriculum of mosque schools was the same as that of regular primary schools.

Conclusions

Management: The project suffered from serious management flaws. The supervisory staff consisted of part time Project Director, two Senior Research Officers one Education Facilitator and one Vocational Supervisor alongwith small supporting staff. The number of villages increased in the project but there had been no increase in the supervisory staff commensurate with the increase in the area of operation. It was necessary to take adequate measures to implement the project effectively with qualified and adequate staff.

Physical Facilities: The successful inputs among the five components were mosque schools and women education centers. Although no enrolment targets were set against which achievements could be measured but the project have considerable impact in the project area. In any future activity of this nature it is imperative that qualitative targets for different activities should be spelled out. One major achievement of the project was that the people of the area gained experience of managing their own affair through the local Village Education Committees. It also created an urge for improvement and a sense of participation and achievement. The beginning was made in right direction which created opportunities for income generating activities. The project also created a self development process for local people.

Cost Effectiveness: It can be said that some components of the project were successful and more cost effective than the others. In the case of mosque school there was no development expenditure on the construction of school so the entire cost of building a two room school was saved. It also increased the enrolment at primary level and brought those children to school who as problem travelling long distance without any public transport. The performance of village workshop cannot be called a success because the skills learned were not used for income generation its laid down expectation. The case of women education centres was cost effective and the cost per trainee was Rs.36/- against Rs.2400/- per trainee in similar centres of other agencies. The Mohallah schools suffered from the lack of similar centres of other agencies. The Mohallah schools suffered from the lack of organizational arrangement hence could not succeed.

The cost of per trainee in women education center was Rs.36/- in village workshop Rs.974/- and in Adult Literacy Centre Rs.116/- which made the project cost effective.

Local Participation: The project was planned in such a way that the local people must be involved and motivated to work for the successful functioning of all the components. The accommodation for women education centres, village workshops, mosque schools and adult literacy was provided by the community. The community was so motivated that, it made some financial contribution to the project in the form of conveyance allowance for two female teachers. These teachers had to travel long distance to reach the project villages. But project certainly faced factional rivalries, tribal/caste differences, political bickerings, religious differences, personal jealousies, extremists idea and inertia. In an future activity of this nature all these factors must be kept in mind at the planning stage of the project.

Income Generation: It was an inherent expectation that this project which adopted non-formal approach to provide variety of skills to village people would be different from the formal education programmes. It was planned that women education centres and village workshops would generate income through the sale of commodities prepared by the trainees. A beginning was made but the impact was very limited because the quality or standard could not be maintained, quantity or production was very slow and small with irregular supply hence the products would not compete with the market. However, the sale criteria was not the only parameter for the success of the project. The project changed the attitude of village people towards education and they were more inclined that this kind of skill training/education should be organized in their villages.

Primary education project

Introduction

The first Primary Education Project partially funded by the World Bank started in 1979 for a period of five years. It was an experimental project with the total cost of US$ 17 million whereas the US$ 10 million were provided by the Bank. The project assisted all the provincial governments and provided classroom buildings, improve teacher training, expand school supervision and improve instructional material. The Primary Education Project was very different from the READ Project. The PEP was for the improvement of primary education under the formal education system and experiment was undertaken in 4000 primary schools covering all provinces of Pakistan. The READ was a non-formal functional adult literacy project.

Objectives

- Increased access to primary schools especially for girls and for rural poor.
- Reduce wastage through the reduction of drop and out and repetition.
- Improved quality of instruction and higher student achievement.
- Reduced unit cost by reducing wastage inherent in drop-out and moving towards larger class and school sizes.

Inputs

Following inputs were provided to the project:

i) Physical facilities
   - Construction of classrooms;
   - Construction of boundary walls of female schools;
   - Construction of residences for female teachers; and
   - Classroom furniture.

ii) Instructional materials
   - Supply of textbooks, teacher's guide books and library books;

- Supply of classroom equipment like teaching kit or agricultural kit; and
- Supply of sport's items for children.

iii) Strengthened Supervision

- Provision of supervisors and a new tier of Learning Coordinators; and
- Provision of mobility for Supervisors and Learning Coordinators.

iv) Added Support to Teachers

- Appointment of Assistant Teachers;
- Establishment of Centre Schools;
- Provision of District Resource Centres; and
- Provision of recurrent type-inservice teachers' training

Strategy

The project was experimental in nature and intended to measure the impact of some inputs to achieve the objectives. The experimentation was *whether* (1) provision of female teacher residences; (ii) availability of assistant teachers can resolve the problem of an inadequate supply of female teachers; particularly in the rural areas; (iii) increased training of teachers result in improved teacher performance and consequent improved pupil achievement; (iv) improved supervision reduces teacher absenteeism; (v) increased contact between parents and teachers results in greater enrolment and less dropout; and (vi) cost per student can be reduced through the used of assistant teachers and movement towards an optimum class and school size.

Measurements to answer these questions were divided into four categories (i) demographic data on population, enrolment dropouts and repetitions secured from school through management channels and school mapping capability; (ii) benchmark tests of pupil achievement and attitudes of parents and community members on education and school; and (iv) cost data.

The project was divided into three periods (i) Preparatory: A period of 20 months devoted primarily to selection and training personnel, construction of physical facilities, and design of experiments. (ii) Experimental School: Years Three school years beginning in March of 1981, 1982, and 1983 in which impact of the project inputs would be measured and evaluated. (iii) Analysis of REsults: A follow-up period of 6 to 9 months in which final experimental results would be analyzed, conclusions drawn and recommendations made.

Achievement Studies: In order to measure improvement in quality it was decided that achievement testing of children should be undertaken starting in 1981 and continuing upto 1984. Data collected during 1981 was to serve as the benchmark. Originally objective tests in 5-6 discipline areas for grade III to V were developed and administered and they were specific to each province. These tests were then modified in the light of feed-back from 1981 and were administered during the second time in 198. On critical perusal these objective tests were found to be extremely deficient and were administered in situations which left much to be desired. Again, the teachers in primary schools went on a strike for three months and the academic years was disrupted. Furthermore, the experimental design did not incorporate control schools. Thus the data on achievement testing collected during 1981 and 1982 had only limited validity for drawing any worthwhile conclusions. The whole strategy was changed then and national tests in mathematics for grade V and science for grade IV were developed. The concept of control schools was also brought in. Thus, the data collected during 1983 served as a benchmark data and comparison with 1984 data led to some meaningful interpretations and conclusions.

Attitudinal Studies: The original experimental design visualized a shift in the attitude towards education on the part of children, parents, teachers and community members as a result of the implementation of the Project. Some attitudinal studies were conducted during 1981 and 1982 in the four provinces using scales specific to provinces. In fact two provinces utilized methodology along the lines of Likert Scales whilst the other two adopted Thurston type of scales. However, after the exercise in 1982 it was felt that the design of attitudinal studies was based on some simplistic assumptions which might be true for a literate community but which were definitely not relevant for the rural areas of Pakistan where literacy was far too low. Besides, the purely academic approach as was imparted to these studies had very little value of a pragmatic nature. The money, energy and time required to undertake these studies was far in excess of any practical use to which the results could be put. Taking into account the very limited research capabilities it was thought expedient to discontinue the activity as proposed originally. The only relevant portion pertained related to the users perception of the efficacy of the various inputs and interventions made under the Project.

Demographic Studies: Demographic Studies were designed to obtain a gain in the participation rate of children or a fall in the dropout rate with consequent impact on unit costs. A computer based demographic questionnaire was designed and data relating to 1981 and

1982 was obtained. It was recommended that the questionnaire was over-ambitious and asked for information which could not possibly be related to the project. Also errors were made during the stage of data entry with the result that the 1981 data was lost for all practical purposes. The data assembled during the cycle 1982 was used as the benchmark data. During 1983 the demographic questionnaire was revised and reduced to one third by keeping only the essential features.

Qualitative Studies: It was felt from the very beginning that data of a quantitative nature though valid and reliable would be of limited value in the type of situation in which an experiment of the scale of the PEP was being undertaken. This depended upon the interpretation of experience and it was often of a fairly subjective dimension. Thus it was thought that some sort of in-depth qualitative studies may be more pertinent in lending illumination to the actual dynamics of the educational process. However, such techniques were fairly new in Pakistan and it was essential first to give researchers adequate training and experience.

Conclusions

The Primary Educational Project was completed in 1984 within its planned five year duration. In this period very useful experiences were gained which could help in the planning of future projects and to make appropriate modification in the structure of education.

Management: The Institutional Framework of the project was too loose and could not ensure its execution effectively as planned. The concept of a team with common objectives and shared aspirations never took deep roots. Several employees who were give on the job training left their jobs or were transferred to other positions. There was considerable turn over in the staff including Chief of the project at federal level and the Project Directors in the provinces. The new incumbents were forced in many ways handicapped because they had to start understanding the project from scratch. Several positions mentioned in the project document and approved by competent authority were not fulfilled. Issues like travelling and daily allowances lingered on unnecessarily and created frustration among the employees. The disbursement claims were not made in time. Similarly the maintenance of accounts was not according to intentional practice of codification. But the project management has to satisfy and fulfill the financial requirements of Federal Government, Provincial Governments and the lending agency, in this case, the World Bank. The researchers were not allowed to go to the field for spot checking of the data from the field. The understanding of the Provincial Project Directors of professional aspect of the project was minimal and they were unable to draw worthwhile lessons of their own from the research and evaluation component. The Provincial Directorates worked in isolation and could not generate community support which was important for the implementation of the project. The government procedures were so intricate and did not help in managing the project. It has become clear from the above that management situation was quite serious and grim for the project. Special procedures need to be worked out for implementing innovative projects of this nature.

Community Support: It is imperative to obtain community support for the successful implementation of any Basic Education programme. This project revealed that energizing and substaining community support was a reciprocal understanding and it should become an explicit strategic objective in the follow on project. It was also established through this project that the attitude of village people had changed considerably towards education because of improved transport facilities, access to newspaper, television, telephone, and a large number of overseas workers. The parents attached highest value to education but with an emphasis that the curriculum should teach to cope with practical problems. The supervision of primary schools were improved through the introduction of new tier of supervisors i.e. learning coordinator. But the project concluded that the primary school supervision should be brought into closer liaison with community institution i.e. Union Councils. The project also demonstrated that where the community was more supportive and enthusiastic the enrolment of children in primary schools and their retention increased between 32.7% to 94.3% within one year between 1982 to 1983.

Physical Facilities: The component of physical facilities was one of the biggest in the project because about 50% of the money was allocated to this category. It was found out through project evaluation that better school buildings, more and properly trained teachers, boundary walls, availability of teaching learning material had direct relationship in encouraging the enrolment and regular attendance of school children. The input of female teacher residences was a failure because in rural culture of Pakistan it was not possible for an unmarried female teacher to live alone in a school which was, in most of the cases, away from the main village. The additional rooms, new boundary walls and in some places new buildings were provided. But all these facilities were supplied in a piece meal fashion without any attempt to ensure that the provision was made at the places of greatest need. The project provided buildings here, tats there, furniture differentially and teacher's residences occasionally. In spite of these problems the additional classroom facility was a distinct success.

Teachers: The teacher of primary schools by and large did not understand the content of the curriculum. It was not because of the lack of professional qualification but even with professional qualification they could hardly teach children. The project envisaged inservice training for teachers but due to the poor implementation, this training could not be provided. In some cases the teacher training was imparted but only for two/three days whereas project document it was planned for at least three weeks. The project concluded that teacher training was the most important element to bring any qualitative changes in primary education.

Supervision: The intervention of Learning Coordinator in the supervisory cadre of primary education was a considerable success. By the large it reduced significantly teacher absenteeism, increased the professional profile and aspirations of primary teachers, ensured a facility for teachers to share their problems are provided in some cases improved model of teaching. This did not mean that learning coordinators input was problem free. It was very difficult for the regular school management to accept learning coordinator as a part of supervisory structure because he was considered a threat to a stereotyped inspection. The learning coordinator taught and practiced the concept of professional supervision - a threat to inertia and incompetence. However the project suggested that it was necessary to establish a compatible working relationships with the administrative structure of the formal system.

Teaching Learning Material: Some learning material was provided to the project schools which included textbooks teaching kits, charts, and guide book for teachers. It was surprising to note that no systematic attempt was made to measure, in any objective way, the contribution of learning materials had made to children's achievement or to evaluate the quality of materials.

The major recommendation of the evaluation report of the primary education project that a follow-up project was necessary to ensure the momentum of this experiment. The experiences and expertise obtained through the project was to be put to effective use for the next project of this nature.

Nai roshni schools

Introduction

Universalization of primary education has been a cherished objective of all the educational policies of Pakistan. The National Educational Policy laid special emphasis on adult and non-formal education. It has been recognized that the formal education system alone cannot meet the challenge of the universalization of education due to limited financial resources and other pressing demands. The target dates to achieve universal primary enrolment for boys 1979 and for girls by 1984 according to the education policy seemed impossible to be achieved. The Government of Pakistan, Ministry of Education, therefore, shifted the target dates to 1987 for boys and 1992 for girls.

In view of the difficulties and problems of access to children, an innovative programme of Nai Roshni schools was started. These kinds of programme have been successfully tried in some regional countries under the name of 'Drop-In' schools. In view of their experience the Nai Roshni Schools were started and operated in the existing primary school buildings in the afternoon because the buildings were not used. Full time teachers were employed to teach a condensed two year primary education curriculum. The programme intended to promote primary education and literacy through formal schooling.

Objectives

The Nai Roshni Schools were planned to achieve following objectives:

- To promote literacy rate by 50% by 1990 under the then Prime Minister's Five Point Programme.
- To provide a second chance to primary school dropouts.
- To increase access to school for those who could not go to primary schools for any reason.
- To provide primary education to higher age group through a condensed course of two years.

Strategy

The programme was launched in March, 1987. It was proposed to open 22,000 such schools over 3 cycles of 2 years each. This would aggregate to a target of 1.65 million students of 10-14 age group including boys and girls according to local needs. Over the first 3 years of implementation, the project would be experimental subject to formative evaluation. It was proposed that existing primary school buildings would be utilized for Nai Roshni schools thus generating, in a complementary way, resources for the school to cover repairs, maintenance and the development of materials. Twenty five students were to be enrolled in each school from different and varying backgrounds. Full time teachers were employed. It was anticipated that most of students enrolled would be from groups identified either as drop-outs or previously non-enrolled.

The Nai Roshni Schools offered to complete the 5 years primary school course in 2 years, which necessitated a set of textbooks, appropriate learning materials and innovative teaching methods. The 25 students recruited were divided into 4, 5 or 6 groups depending on the heterogeneity of ability, necessitating sub-group or individual teaching. There would be no summer vacation, although the schools were to be closed, for short periods only, during the sowing and harvesting seasons. The Nai Roshni pupils therefore would attend their school for 260 days a year, compared with the 180 days a year of children in the formal system.

The Nai Roshni Schools started functioning under a Resident Directorate in each Province, District Project Manager Office in each District with its branches, i.e. Tehsil Literacy Office in each Tehsil. In this way, five Resident Director Offices, 85 District Project Manager Offices, and seven Offices in FATA were established to run this programme under the administrative control of Literacy and Mass Education Commission.

Conclusions

The Nai Roshni Schools were evaluated after one year i.e. 1988. It was not possible to measure the student achievement because the first cycle of the programme was of two years duration. However, the quantitative evaluation revealed that 98.2% of the total schools physically existed.

The most common among those were Government schools. Almost 75% of the Nai Roshni Schools had facilities like Sign-Board, Teacher's Chair, Table, Desks and Mats available. As regards the Admission/Withdrawal registers 83% were maintaining the registers.

It was noticed that at the national level 93.5% teachers were physically present at the school premises. However, in overall comparison, teachers were physically present in 100% in AJK whereas the situation was somewhat different as regards the Nai Roshni Schools of Sindh and NWEP Province. Only 9% of the total teachers had the qualifications of P.T.C. 87.1% of the teachers indicated that they had received training arranged by LAMEC. At the national level 74.3% of the teachers belonged to the same community whereas in Sindh 61% and in NWFP 66.1% of the teachers belonged to the same community.

As regards the drop-outs, it was noticed that it differed from month to month and province. Most of the students attending the school were also enrolling in the age group of 15-19 and 20 years.

It was found that Nai Roshni Schools were being supervised and that supervisors had paid visits to the schools. However, supervisors were not paying the visits so frequently as was required of them in Nai Roshni Schools Project. Only 45.2% paid more than 3 visits in one month and 47.6% in another month.

The training of community representatives as well as the students ranked the Nai Roshni Schools Project very high across all provinces.

Students enrolled were also found in the age group of 15-19 and 20 years old. It could, therefore, be concluded that though the age limit in the present Nai Roshni Schools Project was fixed 10-14 years, students had been enrolled on the request of the community. Students above fourteen years old might not approach the schools simply when they knew the age limit fixed in the programme. There was fast turn over in enrollments in the Nai Roshni Schools. Every month some new students seek admission and some old ones dropped out.

The "Nai Roshni" was not entirely a new concept. This kind of schooling had been working in several countries with success. There was no country that has dropped the programme after commencement. It went on with modifications with special emphasis on supervision and back up services.

IQRA Pilot project

Introduction

The IQRA Pilot Project was launched in October 1986 in the Districts of Islamabad and Rawalpindi under the administration of Literacy and Mass Education Commission. Prior to this project, several programmes of adult literacy were launched but the success rate was minimal. The literacy rate could not increase by 0.5% each year whereas the annual population growth rate was 3.1%. There were several reasons for the failure of literacy programmes. Some of those were (i) lack of motivation; (ii) out dated administrative structure; (iii) defective teaching techniques; (iv) lack of teaching-learning material and above all; (v) lack of resources.

Objectives

The concept of the IQRA Pilot Project was a simple and direct approach to the problem. A literate, irrespective of his or here qualification, could volunteer and join the scheme to teach any number of illiterates, in his or her own time, and bring them to an acceptable level of literacy. The scheme aimed at producing 50,000 illiterates in one year from one district of federal territory of Islamabad, at a cost of Rs.1150 per literature.

The other objectives of the project were as follows:

- To adopt an approach based on monetary incentive to the teacher which would compel him in accomplishing his goal.
- To vector the energies of literates and illiterates of in one direction i.e. the struggle for the eradication of illiteracy as national movement.
- To evolve a strategy based on totally indigenous experiences without recoursing to any foreign model, so that a workable and economical solution could be found for the eradication of illiteracy in Pakistani environment.
- Since past efforts based on person to person contact or motivation through mass media have very successful, a cadre of self interested motivators to solve the problem was created.

Strategy

Despite the simplicity of the concept the strategy was perforce complex and stringent. The main components were as follows:

- The plan was predominantly result-oriented because it rewarded a teacher handsomely for the labour/effort he or she put-in, to make one or more persons literate.

- Emphasis on the monitoring of the scheme was an extra-ordinary feature of the project, concept and plan. The teacher who volunteered had to prove the credentials of the illiterate(s) presented as candidate(s) qualified through a prescribed test for becoming literate(s).
- In order to catch the imagination of the masses, the plan was based on an intensive motivation campaign with the help of-the mass media.
- It envisaged evoking awareness and mass response from the people for accelerating the pace of literacy drive in the country.
- The programme wanted to develop a technique which fully tool into consideration the national social trends, aspirations and above all the adverse effect of mass illiteracy on the socio-economic development.

Conclusions

1) The Iqra Pilot Project overwhelmingly attracted females to become literate. This reflects very clearly that the cultural attitudes towards female education are very positive for the development of education in rural areas.
2) In spite of the fact that the project was for adult illiterates but it attracted relatively younger age group between 9-20 years which comprised 59.49% of those who enrolled in the project.
3) 65% adult literates who enrolled in the project belonged to rural areas and 35% were from urban areas.
4) Time taken to literate a person varied from one month

to more than six months. 20.42% of the neo-literate took three months to acquire the literacy skills, while 33.76% took 6 months and 40.24% spent more than 6 months to become literate.

5) The most effective motivational campaign was through T.V. and Radio followed by peer group influence and relatively small number of illiterates decided on its own to join the project.

6) Only 12% of the neoliterates tool the oath that they were illiterate before joining Iqra Pilot Project.

7) Another 12% also produced either identity cards with thump impression that can be interpreted as indicator of their illiteracy or Form-B of their parents registration which also pointed out their illiteracy status.

8) Approximately 11% of the parents testified about the illiteracy of their wards.

9) 65% of the people could not provide any evidence prescribed by the evaluation team of their "illiteracy status" prior to joining the project.

10) 82% neo-literates could read and write the minimum level prescribed by the evaluation team but as 65% enrolled in the programme assumed to be literate hence the literacy ratio of neo-literates was not more than 17%.

The project was not properly implemented and serious deficiencies were found in its monitoring. There was no convincing evidence that the majority of students enrolled in the project were illiterate before joining the project.

Conclusions

1. Implementation

One of the major findings of this case study is the poor implementation of different Education Programmes/ Projects. This is because of over rigidity of the system which does not allow mid stream adjustments or modifications. The IQRA Project was badly implemented and serious deficiencies were found in its monitoring. The achievement claimed by Literacy & Mass Education Commission were far below the proclaimed figures. The actual number made literate through the project at best was 17% or 2780 persons. The financial expenditure on this activity was Rs. 5881/- per illiterate instead of Rs.1150/- as originally calculated in he project. In READ Project, a part time Project Director was appointed all through the duration of the programme. He had to perform several other responsibilities hence could not concentrate on the proper implementation of the project. Three out of the four projects under analysis were delayed which increased escalation costs of the programmes. In the PEP by and large the Project Directors in he provinces did not allow its staff to go to the field to monitor the implementation of the project. The Nai Roshni School programme was better implemented and the quantitative evaluation revealed very positive results. The programme was discontinued for the reasons best known to the authorities.

2. Management

It is a matter of common knowledge that the management skills of middle level administrators in the education sector are extremely limited. This was evident from the PEP in which the management framework was too lose and could not ensure its execution effectively. The concept of team with common objectives and share aspiration did not take place. Several employees who were given on the job training left their jobs or were transferred to other positions. In the IQRA Pilot Project the managerial laxities wasted scarce resources. It was clearly laid down in the project document that only illiterate persons will only be registered with Literacy and Mass Education Commission. But it turned out that 65% of those who enrolled as illiterates were already literates. The fake registration was a major management flaw. The Nai Roshni Schools also suffered problems. As these schools were operating in the afternoon in the existing primary school buildings which created rivalry over authority and responsibility. The appointment of teachers were made on political basis hence the competence and merit were ignored. In the project READ number of villages were increased in the project but there was no increase in supervisory staff commensurate with the increase in the area of operation. The lack of qualified and inadequate staff posed a serious management problem.

3. Planning

The planning by and large of four projects have been sporadic and not based on adequate research. In the PEP female teacher residences were constructed in some of the experimental schools with the intentions that teachers would stay there hence the teacher absenteeism will be reduced. But it was not fully researched that in Pakistan rural culture it is not possible for an unmarried female to live in school accommodation without proper protection and particularly when most of the schools, were the residences were built, were away from the main village. Similarly the transport facilities were provided for supervision. But it was not envisaged that the transport for the project has to be obtained through international bidding which involves complicated and long procedures. This input was delayed by two years in a five years project. As a result the impact of one of the major inputs was not properly studied. While planning Nai Roshni Schools the provincial governments were neither consulted nor taken into confidence. They did not own the programme which was to be implemented in the provincial primary schools. Similarly the planning of Nai Roshni was done in such way to make this effort as an employment project instead of education project. In the IQRA project which provided financial incentive of Rs.1000/- for teacher to make one person literate but there was no financial motivation for illiterate. The planning of READ project was over ambitious. The number of components could be three instead five/six. The planning of most of the project was done without obtaining enough information from the expected project areas and clientele.

4. Monitoring

Every project document does refer to the importance of monitoring for the successful implementation of the projects. No explicit mechanism was provided to monitor the project except that the utilization of funds were monitored only to satisfy the bureaucracy that the money was spent. Whether the expenditure make on the component as planned, was less important. The monitoring in these projects were done irregularly and in non-professional ways. In READ project the supervisory staff was occasional visitors to the project site only with a purpose of bureaucratic inspection. In the primary education project monitoring system was better probably because the lending agency, World Bank, was strict in this regard. In spite of that the project staff was quite reluctant to leave the provincial capitals whereas the project schools were in rural areas and difficult terrains. In the IQRA pilot adequate transport facilities were provided for monitoring, however the use was misdirected which was proved from the results i.e. 65% literates were registered as illiterates in the project.

5. Resource constraint

In a developing country like Pakistan the financial and technical resources are limited and likely to remain so in future. Interestingly enough none of the four projects which have been analyzed suffered from any financial resources constraints but still the success rate was modest. Only Primary Education Project has been expanded on large scale with some modifications whereas the IQRA Project, Nai Roshni Schools and READ Project have been abandoned so far. There have been delays in the releases of funds but the management problems were quite serious during the implementation of the projects. It was not only the scarcity of the financial resources but the poor management of resources were responsible for wastage. The funds have three stages which include allocations, releases and expenditure. Usually the allocations have been referred as the funds available for the program but most of the time releases are not made either because of lack of funds at a particular time or procedural and codal formalities are so rigid that whatever little was available lapses. The releases sometimes were not fully backed by the appropriate expenditure in the right direction and for that particular programme. It was not uncommon to spend the money of one head against the other which will easily absorb the funds and make it visible e.g. purchase of vehicle instead building a two room school.

The four projects in the case study did not confront serious delays in financial releases. It may be interesting to note that several lending and donor agencies have provided more than half billion US Dollars for Basic Education with a thrust on Primary Education. The World Bank ended US$ 217.5 million, Asian Development Bank gave a loan US$ 64.4 million, United States Agency for International Development provided grant in aid of US$ 280 million, UNICEF US$ 5.2, CIDA C$ 19.24 and some other small grants have been received. This entire amount of money became available and is to be expanded within the next 8 years. It is strongly urged that financial resources are available but their use has to efficient and effective.

6. Research and development

The planning of education in Pakistan is more prone to social stratification than social mobility, partly because the planners apprehend that the outdated education system which is in practice won't accept any innovations or changes. But this does not deter the planners to suggest structural changes in the system, to redistribute educational opportunities and bring qualitative orientation in the Basic Education Programmes.

4

Non-formal Education Materials and their Revision

Educational Materials had to be prepared for those who teach as well as for adults who are exposed to literacy for the first time in their lives. It was indeed not difficult to produce the teaching materials for the instructors. But the 'Learning tools' for the participants had to be designed, tested and evaluated with great care in the form of posters, photographs, models and written lessons. Conventional textbooks and urban-oriented posters and photographs could have no relevance in carrying the message of this programme to the intended participants. The entire success of the programme depended on this single problem of intelligibility and suitability of the visual material on which discussion could be initiated between the teacher and the taught.

Discussion guide in Telugu

A discussion guide in Telugu entitled Mother Child Welfare Education (Mata Sisu Samkshema Vidya) was prepared in the Workshop for use in non-formal education classes by health Educators. It was designed to help them and the women participants during the discussion period of about 45 minutes. Subjects dealt with in this guide included:

- need for a pregnant woman to have a medical check-up:
- nutritional requirements of a pregnant and lactating woman:
- nutrition of the infant and the toddler.

In addition to the Discussion Guide, the Health Educators (Auxiliary Nurse Midwives) who were the teachers of non-formal education in mother child centres were given the following materials:

(i) Teaching material for non-formal education (in Telugu): This was intended to be a source book of information on the subject matter. It contained 47 lessons classified under eight chapters, covering 18 topics of the course content.

(ii) Food and health (in Telugu): This was a publication of the National Institute of Nutrition, Hyderabad, and was meant to be used by the Health Educators as reference material.

(iii) A Manual of Nutrition for Auxiliary Nurse Midwives: This was a handbook for use in the training of ANMS.

Visual aids

Owing to the absence of electricity in most of the villages selected for project operation and the high cost of projectors and other audio-visual equipment, it was decided that only manually operated visual aids would be used in non-formal education and functional literacy classes. Accordingly, prior to the holding of the workshop for preparation of materials, one set of visuals, mainly charts and posters, already available in the country from various sources, were collected and displayed in the Workshop. We had, indeed, a large stock of posters, but none of these had been sent into the field testing. The Consultant started sending the suitable ones into the field along with the lesson units and then she personally supervised the classes to determine the communication value of the posters.

The visuals performed two distinct functions: (1) lending colour to the drab class-rooms as well as arousing the interest of the participants: (2) Helping specifically in introducing a topic for discussion. As the posters were not prepared specially for the project, they performed the first function more effectively than the second. With the help of a Consultant on visual aids for non-formal education, these were reviewed in the light of the course content.

In addition to the posters and charts. The book Birth Atlas, several photographs and selected illustrations designed in the Workshop were also used in the project. The Consultant, who was specially appointed for testing and evaluation of materials, worked with the project Officers at Mahbubnagar and designed a procedure for testing the photographs.

Testing Photographs: About 20 photographs were tested. The investigators visited the villages and randomly selected 10 women to test the effectiveness of the photographs, using the following procedure. They were to show one photograph at a time to one respondent and then ask the question: 'What do you see in this photograph?' The reply was recorded verbatim.

In respect of some visuals, identification by the respondent will be simple and direct as in the case of the picture of a baby being given a bath. Here, the job is done without further questioning. But with certain other photographs, identification may not be easy. For example, in photograph No.5, a likely answer might be 'picture of a woman holding a girl'. Then the question would be: 'Does the child look normal?' If the answer is 'Yes, the answer is recorded. If the answer is 'No', the next question would be: 'What do you think is the matter with the child?'

The information received in Telugu was then translated into English and the content analysed. If out of ten respondents, 7-9 identified the picture correctly, it was decided that the photograph concerned could be used. On the basis of this 10-12 photographs were selected. Later, during phase II, a photographer was commissioned to take 6 sets of photographs, each set containing 6-10 pieces. Considerable amount of time was spent in planning the kinds of photographs needed for easy assimilation. A number of these were mounted on card board for use in the classes.

Other visuals

As the visuals started going into the field, there was a demand for more. Flip charts obtained from Lucknow were given to the teachers with very clear instructions on the manner in which to use them. Later classes were personally supervised by the consultant in order to determine the effectiveness of the flip charts. Some skepticism had been expressed regarding the effectiveness of a flip chart on 'the importance of weaning foods'. It was said that in differences the locals and dress patterns would cause an interference in the understanding of the visual. It was further suggested that the flip chart should be adapted to suit the local scene. The suggestion was valid but for lack of artistic talent in Hyderabad, no solution appeared to be in sight. Therefore, it was decided to test them and the flip charts were sent into the field.

The teacher was asked to flip it once over without saying anything. As she did so, the remarks of participants included comments on the colour of the clothes, the manner in which the women were dressed, etc. When the teacher flipped it over the second time, the extraneous details were forgotten and the women started noticing the main point of the flip chart, namely, the difference between a weaned child and a breast-fed child. The third time over, the message of the flip chart was stated by the participants in very clear and definite terms.

This pattern of responses was followed in all the mother child centres. The visuals thus tested in a classroom situation were posters, flip charts, flannel-graphs, sketches, drawings and models. In view of the enthusiastic response of the participants, some more visuals were developed and used so as to provide the participants stimulating and interesting sessions.

Visual support

For visual support of lesson units on "Food Beliefs" (hot, cold food, etc.) small packets containing a small quantity of pulses and cereals or small pieces of fruits and vegetables which the participants considered harmful for pregnant or lactating mothers were put on display. Later, the women built a flannel-graph with the 'food packets' that had been supplied to the centres. The participant response to this method was encouraging: for at last some, the identification of some of the taboo foods had not been very clear earlier.

The use of the materials prepared for non-formal education in phase I and their revision began almost simultaneously when action programme began in July 1973 and continued up to April 1974. Forty-five lesson units covering the following subject areas in the course content were prepared: Health care of Toddler: Child Development and Rearing Practices: Responsible Parenthood: General Knowledge: and Civics and Citizenship. These unites were tried out in the field and were found to be quite effective. The visual aids collected or improvised locally were used along with these lessons. It was felt that the visuals were insufficient in number. The umber was increased in phase II.

Discussion session

The field observation made during this period, though meagre and limited, were enough to show that 30 to 40 minutes was optimal time for a discussion session. In the light of these observations, the lessons prepared for use in phase I during February and March 1974 required considerable pruning.

Further the language used in writing the lessons, though simple and in spoke form, did not conform to the local dialect. Consequently, further simplification of the language used in the lesson units became necessary. There was a noticeable reluctance to discuss the subject of Family Planning and this was reflected in the lack of enthusiasm among the women even to hear a story related by the instructor.

Revision of materials in phase II

During phase II, 100 non-formal education lessons were taught, covering the following five subject areas of the course content:

1. Material and health care for a healthy baby:
2. Child development and rearing practices:
3. Health care of infants and toddlers:
4. Responsible parenthood; and
5. General knowledge which includes services available through government departments and citizenship rights.

Out of the 100 lessons, the Project Officer (materials) supervised forty-five of them during his inspection visits to the centres. His personal observations made during the 69 inspection visits enabled him to gather information relating to: (i) the capacity of the participants to receive, assimilate and use the knowledge gained by them through the lessons: (ii) the inherent handicaps which arise on account of the social and economic conditions in which the participants live: and (iii) the capacity shown by the Health Educators/literacy Teachers to understand the information contained in the lessons and the grasp they exhibited during the transmission of massages conveyed by the materials. These three important considerations helped greatly in deciding the scope and magnitude of the quantum of knowledge, the essential practice that should be chosen for transmission through these materials and the methodology that should be adopted for the purpose.

It was realised that the capacity of the participants to understand, assimilate and practice the knowledge gained was very much limited and conditioned by their traditional beliefs and the poverty in which they were steeped and by their philosophy of life. These field observations suggested that the lessons should not be loaded with informations of purely academic importance. On the other hand, it was realised that they would be very well received if a few practical and practicable suggestions only were given as messages in the lessons.

Guidelines for revision

Feedback reports also provided some useful information to rationalise the revision of materials. On the basis of 12 feedback reports received in phase II, materials including visuals were revised. Materials were also revised on the basis of tests conducted to determine the amount of information gained and retained by participants. The number of participants answering a question correctly was taken roughly as an index of the degree of acceptance of the message. The information was used in improving some of the lessons.

Similarly, the answers given by 141 participants from 12 centres in the final assessment conducted in February 1975, after all the subject areas had been covered, were also analysed. The results indicated that 17 messages required increased emphasis while 12 could be retained as they were and that addition of two new items in the lessons was required.

In the course of the final revision of the lessons used in the non-formal education project due consideration was given to the level and intelligibility of the language used and the methodology followed in the lessons. Sources materials used in phase I were revised for use in the preparation of lessons for phase II. Sources material on child development and rearing practices was prepared by the professor of child development, college of home sciences, Hyderabad, and this was modified by the project officer (materials) to suit the local conditions. Source material on general knowledge and information about services were obtained from the publications of the Andra pradesh information department. Agricultural department and the agricultural university.

Every care was taken to use simple, non academic but idiomatic Telugu in the particular local dialect as the medium.

5

Non-Formal Education in the Setting of Higher Education

Role of universities in higher education

Education after secondary stage of formal education is generally denoted as higher education. This is also called tertiary stage. Several types of institutions are engaged in the process of higher education. The universities occupy a unique position in this enterprises and are at the pinnacle of higher education and have a pivotal role to play in a country. They are autonomous bodies with or without state government's funds-according to the political ideology of the country. From the time the universities were established-even during the time of Nalanda and Taxila in ancient India-they are able to set trends in the society. It is all the more significant now. The universities like Oxford, Cambridge, Sorbonne, Harvard, Yale and Leningrad are world renowed as they are able to set the tone of theoretical discussions in various fields of natural sciences, social sciences and humanities. They are the acknowledged leaders in the field of higher education. Till recent times the universities stood aloof interested in expanding the frontiers of knowledge and serving an elite and not about the requirements of common man. The objectives and the role of the universities are undergoing changes. Alternative channels are slowly making inroads in university education. These changes in universities are traced with special references to the universities in India. The origin of present day universities in India could be traced from medieval universities of Europe and Britain as the first Indian universities were modelled after London University. These universities were transplantations by the British rulers of India and did not get any nourishment in the early stages from indigenous culture. They have no roots nor did they desire any inspiration either in structure or curriculum from Nalanda or Taxila.

The objectives of education and that of higher education have undergone vast change today from what they were in British India. During these thirty seven years from 1947 tremendous changes have taken place on all fronts and fields in India as in the rest of the world. The rising of independent nations and general awareness of developing and less developed countries have brought home the need to experiment with new methods in all fields including that of education. The concept of life-long education has captured the imagination of intellectuals and commoners alike. The university has to take the challenge of making this a reality. In this environment the spread of education by non-formal means like the correspondence education has assumed great significance. A review of the origin, the aims and functions of universities from their inception to the present day will make it easier to comprehend the immense changes taking place in the universities.

Evolution of the universities in Europe

The modern universities have their genesis in the twelfth

century universities of Europe which catered to the people who could pursue knowledge for its own sake-to people who are interested in disinterested pursuit of knowledge. Later on from the medieval period i.e., from fourteenth century onwards, the universities came under the fold of the catholic church. The universities in those days were supranational in a sense. "The very work 'university' denoted in ancient Bologna the society of foreign students, associating themselves into 'nations': Ultramontane, Lombard, Tuscan and Roman." Students could migrate from one university to another. They spoke the same language, Latin. The students in the universities formed an international community. Ashby maintains that the peoples of Europe in those days united in an intellectual solidarity that they have never since regained. The graduates were trained theologians, lawyers or physicians and occupied positions of responsibility in the church and the state. At the end of fifteenth century, University of Paris became a power in a sense that the ideas flowing there influenced and guided the policies of that time. Sometimes there were dissensions and quarrels. The universities.

> Contributed an intellectual common-wealth embodying the same ideal, fulfilling the same function exchanging students and ideas. The great contribution to society was as Rushdall said universities placed the administration of human affairs...in the hands of educated men.

European universities in 19th century

Any University tried to live upto its ideal and at the same time tries to be socially relevant. Renaissance and later reformation brought a number of changes. By the 19th century the catholic church lost its hold and the solidarity of the earlier centuries was thereby lost. The universities were in turmoil and underwent changes as nation states came into prominence when loyalty to the state replaced implicit faith in the church. For example, in France under Napoleon, the supremacy of the state was unquestioned and hence the influence of the universities diminished. In Italy a number of small states came into existence and the university got splintered. But in England and Germany, the universities adapted themselves to new social conditions. Germany introduced a new dimension into the set-up of a university as a research body, teacher surrounded by disciples-resembling the Indian gurukul. The teacher's function in that set-up is not only to discuss but to be in a perpetual quest for truth.

Objectives of universities in 19th century

The aims of universities in England and Scotland and the U.S.A. prevalent at that time gives an idea about the objectives with which the British established in a subject nation like India and on what lines the universities developed. In Cambridge and Oxford there was no professional faculties of theology, law or medicine; they concentrated on faculty of arts which was a prerequisite for any professional course in those days. There was no disinterested pursuit of knowledge in the form of research. These institutions provided an all-round education for a privileged class. The new foundations in England in 19th century like university of Manchester and colleges associated with university of London took utilitarian approach and included technological subjects as they were relevant to the bourgesie of England immediately after the Industrial Revolution. Scottish universities, on the other hand retained the faculties of theology, law and medicine to which a number of students were admitted every year. "There was no effort to superpose character-training on the formal teaching, or to cultivate the qualities of leadership; the universities offered learning to the rank and file of the people." The Scottish university was adapted to the social environment and poor students could also get admission. Study was sandwiched between the annual cycle of crops and terms were fixed so as to suit the agricultural year. In Oxford and Cambridge people arrived by coaches being mostly children of upper classes while in Scottish universities, they came walking. Oxford and Cambridge were insulated by Anglicanism, Scotland maintained contact with other universities, especially those of Holland. German universities taught meticulous accuracy, Oxford and Cambridge taught students to be reasonable and conform to the life of a gentleman of leisure, Scottish universities gave students a durable set of moral principles.

The European (Spanish) proto-type universities got transplanted first in Latin America. The course of their history was different. The first transplantation of university from England occurred in North America-in British colonies of that time. It was Harvard and modelled on Cambridge University-especially the laws, liberties and orders. But this university had no constraints and was free to adopt or dissent from the practices of higher education in Britain. The migrants could do what they wanted. It is a paradox that the puritan fathers having escaped from political persecution of England created rigidity of moral values. On the other hand Yale, Brown and Rutgers in the U.S.A. were orthodox instruments of community and faith. In the U.S. There is a lay control as against academic control and community has a say in the functioning of the universities from the beginning of their inception. The 'democratization of the curriculum' started in U.S.A. in

Cornell University. Greek was introduced with the renaissance, natural sciences with the enlightenment, technology at the tail-end of the industrial revolution. Mass education has its beginnings in America. It might have dulled sensitivity to quality in some universities but it has in no way hindered high quality product and growth of centres of excellence. The innovation is a necessity in 19th century America, as it is now in developing and less developed countries. Young America had no use for 'scholarly elites', the social pressure acting on a system of higher education in U.S.A. Produced land-grant colleges, which are the unique contribution of the U.S.A. to the broadening role of universities.

Transplantation of British University system in India

We shall now turn to a study of what types of universities were transplanted to the India soil. Britain did not consider as to what type of university would suit the Indian conditions. Instead she wanted the Indian University to be fascimile of a University of England. Hence the highly research-oriented universities in Germany or centralised or articulated educational system of Frances was not considered. In Latin America the universities were started under the aegis of the Church and King of Spain. In North America the emigrants themselves started the universities-of course based on universities in England. In countries like Japan the government itself imported western higher education for modernisation. In India the British Government transplanted the British system. At that time in England there were five generic types of universities. There were no clearly enuncited "principles of higher education, as in the present day. London University was taken as the model (which was created in 1836). It was established solely to conduct examination in the outlying colleges and award degrees. It did not start teaching till 1900. It conducted examinations to external students from any institute approved by the Privy Council in any part of the British Empire or within territories under the Government of East India Company. But the curriculum in London was novel-after two years of study B.A. degree was given on the results of a single examination and a further two years study was required for M.A. degree. In the curriculum mathematics and classics formed the hard core of the examination. Botany, chemistry and animal physiology were introduced as optional subjects. Degrees in science subjects were introduced in 1860. Further it was non-sectarian.

Birth of Indian Universities

Wood's despatch was prepared by East India Company for its educational policy. The despatch provided for the constitution of universities in India. A senate was constituted with members appointed by the Privy Council. Three universities in Calcutta, Bombay and Madras were established in 1856. The fundamental aim of these universities was of diffusing "the improved arts, science, philosophy and literature of Europe". The main emphasis was on European learning and the Indian heritage was brushed aside inn the university. The special oriental institutions supported by East India Company continued under a separate status and oriental studies were not included in the new found universities. medical course and legal course presented no problems-british system was followed-except in the legal course, Muncipal law and positive law were included by the universities. The arts course was different from the English model. English was compulsory and one Indian language (or Vernacular) has t be taken. The subject in the curriculum were mathematics, natural philosophy, physical sciences, mental and moral sciences. A degree could be obtained after matriculation by attending four years of college. Somehow the universities did not attain the academic standards of London University. Wood's despatch conceived the university with the aim of transmitting an alien culture. The students coming out of the university have to be eligible for government service was another aim for establishing universities. In this aim the universities proved successful. As time progressed some of the university's narrowness was removed and a number of disciplines were added.

Role of the Indian Universities

In the beginning the university's role was to hold examinations for the colleges in its jurisdiction. Gradually they became teaching institutions. Indian languages, oriental learning and philosophy was not included in the university curriculum till half a century later. In 1920s they became research bodies. The main problem faced by the universities can be expressed in the words of Sir Eric Ashby.

> To exclude from university studies for half a century the whole of oriental learning and religion and purvey to Hindus and Muslims a History and Philosophy whose roots lie exclusively in the Mediterranean and in Christianity, to communicate the examinable skeleton of European Civilization without ensuring that the values and standards which give flesh to those bones are communicated too, to set up the external paraphernalia of an University without the warmth fellowship of

> academic society; those are the handicaps against which India Universities are still struggling and which prevent the University from becoming the Centre and focus of India's intellectual life.

The universities increased from three at the time of inception to 20 in 1947 when India gained its independence. All the universities more or less followed the same pattern. Banaras Hindu University (in 1916 and Aligarh Muslim University (in 1920) were specialty established to highlights the culture of the respective communities under the aegis of the centre. Even though oriental learning very heavily on western concepts. Still with all the draw-backs, higher education succeeded in awakening in the people the need to strive for democracy and flight the British. Education was titled towards arts (or liberal education) and there was disproportionate number of lawyers. (It is of interest to note here that Britain after her experience in India never started universities in other colonies as they didn't want disgruntled subjects.

Aims of University Education in India

After independence the goals of higher education took definite shape. The need to reform the university education in India became essential and urgent in order to achieve a break form the legacy of the colonial past. But as there were apprehensions in revamping the entire system at one stroke, changes were introduced gradually. The goals of new India have no ambiguity. The newly formed government of India set up a commission to go into the problems of university education in India under Radhakrishnan as the chairman. The report came out in 1949. As stated in this report it is for the universities to create knowledge and train minds who would bring together the two-" material resources and human energies." The university is

> to provide a coherent picture of the universe and an integrated way of life. We must obtain through it a synophic vision, asynoptic vision a 'samanvaya' of different items of knowledge" (University Commission Report, 1949).

The university education is to produce cultured people. Here culture is taken as intellectual alertness, receptiveness to beauty, humane feelings and social enthusiasm. In the same report it is said that the universities should act as the organs of civilization-i.e., universities have to train and nurture the intellectual who can guide the country. People have strive for an integrated education. Education should produce knowers of self, 'atmavit' and not just knowers of tests 'mantravit'. Education has to be considered as growth. What Cardinal Newsman said in 1852 is of relevance even today. The function of the university continues "to be training good members of society". Indian education has to strive to provide social justice, keeping the dignity of the individual in an environment of democracy. The same aims and objectives of higher education were once again delved deep into in the Indian Education Commission Report of 1964-66 and reiterated. The commission delineates the aims as

> to seek and cultivate new knowledge, to engage vigorously and fearlessly in the pursuit of truth and to interpret old knowledge and beliefs in the light of new needs and discoveries...to strive to promote equality and social justice and to reduce social and cultural differences through diffusion

> of education-foster in the teachers and students and through them in society generally, the attitudes and values needed for developing the good life in individuals and society.
>
> The Indian universities in particular should
>
> learn to serve as the conscience of the nation, they should encourage individuality, variety and dissent with in a climate of tolerance-they should develop programmes of adult education in big way.

When Indian Education Commission gave its report, the number of universities rose to 64 in 1996, 108 in 1984. At the present there are 179 some of the universities are residential and some affiliating ones. There are certain established disciplines and some old universities are retaining their pre-eminence and the new universities are trying to catch up. The Kothari Commission has clearly states

> At present 'Centre of gravity' of Indian academic life is largely outside India. That is to say, our scholars and scientists working in fields which are internationally cultivated still tend to look outside India for judgment of their work, for intellectual models of the problems which they study, for the books they read and for their forum of appreciation and approval

This perhaps was one of the chief reasons for the universities not able to take up the challenges of Indian society. India has still not recovered completely from her reliance on western institutions. India still looks to them to guide her and solve her problems. India should look at her problems in her socio-logical, economic and political background and not with the coloured glasses of an alien culture which she does not understand completely.

Life long Education in the context of University Education

At this stage it is worthwhile to pose the question "should higher education cater to a favoured few, an elite who will be the trend-setters or to masses? This is the crucial question which is being faced by higher education in the entire world. It is felt that education should not be the prerogative of a few, but should be freely available to all. Education is not something which begins or ends in a class-room. Education is a continuous process which is always in the making; it should be regarded as co-terminus with life itself. Education which is imparted should be life-long. This is not a new concept but it has received world-wide attention. An ideal teacher (according to Indian philosophy and western philosophy) is one who is a life-long student-a 'vidyarthi' in the true sense-a seeker of knowledge. This philosophy of life-long education has been extended to the general public. The International Education Commission 'Learning to Be' has explored the ways and means of making life-long education a possibility and a reality.

In the context of higher education what are the implications of life-long education? Is it the same as opening the possibility of pursuing higher education at any stage in life or on part-time basis or by correspondence? Is life-long education the same as recurrent education, where is possibility of getting education form competent persons and experts in the field one is interested in? Recurrent education has assumed importance in the present technological society where the skills become obsolete rapidly, as new techniques and innovations emerge. This makes the professional to move with times and adapt to the new ways. No, life-long education is something more than that. There will be a conscious effort by a person to learn always. Hence the goal/ideal will be the

> education enterprise will become efficient, just and human by undergoing radical changes affecting the essence of educational action as well as the time and place for education, in short by adopting the concept of life-long education.

It is easy to make the above statement. How can it be practised? Is it the same in developed and developing countries? In the developed countries there is compulsory education for periods varying between 10 and 12 years and there is almost hundred percent enrolment. (It does not necessarily mean that everyone completes secondary education). In a country like U.S.A., higher education is freely accessible to those who come out of secondary education. They can go to universities, four year liberal colleges, and community colleges apart from various technical schools. But not all the people coming out of secondary education are keen to enroll in full-time education. To them an alternative system is better. In countries like the U.S.S.R. part-time education and correspondence education has been used for the benefit of people in the working-force from the says of October revolution. The alternative channels can open up in making education change from a purely utilitarian aspect to something of a more permanent nature. It is hoped that what is said in 'Learning to Be' will become a reality.

In this light, tomorrow's education must form a

> co-ordinated totality in which all sections of society are structurally integrated. It will be universalized and continual. From the point of individual people, it will be total and creative and consequently individualized and self-directed. It well be the bulwark and driving force in culture, as well as in promoting professional activity. This movement is irresistible and irreversible. It is the cultural revolution of our time

It has to be questioned whether the above statement is a utopian vision-or whether it is possible to make such a revolution in education in a reality? If so, how? Several agencies like private trusts, parochial institutions, government contribute to the spread of education. The special contributions which the universities can make with their unique position given to them by the society are discussed. In developing countries like India, even the rudiments of education are not within the reach of millions. But the universities are in a position to bring about changes in several aspects of society. For examples the universities can train special teachers for adult education programmes (which they are doing under the national Adult Education programme).

The changing role of university education in the present times

The primary function of the universities is to be centres of excellence from where new ideas originate. Where leadership qualities take shape and where scientific talents emerge. The question posed is, should the universities remain aloof, keeping the churning out of specialised knowledge as their sole reason for existence and handing them out to a selected few or should they join the mainstream and try to solve the problems of society and make education freely accessible to large numbers. If the first proposition is acceptable, the universities will be shutting off most of their community from the universities' orbit. When the universities were started, they were elite institutes-with admissions limited to a few. The products of these universities were considered the cream of the society. But as time progressed, universities multiplied. Still the access to the universities is restricted and limited (changing from country to country). The egalitarian principle is catching up with everyone and with the increased awareness and rise in the aspirational level of the common man, the university has to respond to the demand of the commoner and not stay in the fringe. Then the second proposition assumes special significance in the present context.

The origin of the university was traced in early part of this chapter. In the beginning of 20th century the role of the universities was that of a 'sanctuary of truth'. The main function of university was a mission to see that values like adhering to strict academic discipline and research were carried. In the renowned universities ,strict and very high standards were maintained. In Britain and European countries admission was restricted to a few and in the recent years it is being liberalized by establishing new universities and institutes of higher education. The danger of established universities is they become conservative and tend to resist change. They are not willing to experiment with new ideas and innovate.

In the present day the newly independent democratic countries have pledged themselves to serve the people and bring them out from a morass of poverty and superstition.

These countries have to be socially responsive to the demands of the people. The universities cannot stand aloof as specialised institutions but should take up the challenge and play their role in the efforts to transform society. Disciplines which help to advance the ideals of society should be developed. They should not be unduly attached to disciplines which have got entrenched but are no longer useful to contemporary society. The individual student should be able to choose from disparate disciplines.

> The underlying philosophy is that education (perhaps at all levels) should no longer be concerned with transmission of a fixed and inherited body of knowledge but rather with the development of competence (vocational and social) of the individual. It is the ability to do that is important rather than the ability to reproduce predetermined quantities of knowledge. The intellectual stimulation becomes a part of the exercise. There-fore the universities, as repository of wisdom, have also to take the mantle of social conscious keepers. The universities need not necessarily uphold only the role of 'sanctuary of truth' including pursuit of scientific truth as an end in itself. Apart from being a mission university, it should strive to become a mirror university, that is to mirror the desires and aspirations of the people and should respond to them. The university has to come to the doorstep of the masses. The external objectives become dominant-i.e., they should provide much needed manpower essential for the political and economic growth of the country.

> These can be called the social-service station or culturemarts. Unlike in the case the 'sanctuary of truth' type universities, the external members and community will have the voice on the activities of the universities and the wishes of students will be taken into account.

The IEC envisaged that the non-academic element i.e., members of the community will be able to exert considerable influence thought not actually impose their views.

> The representation of the non-academic element on university bodies should be mainly for the purpose of presenting the wider interests of society as a whole to the university but not to improve them.

Imposition by any one, be it a scholar or a politician, can bring no positive results. The upward flow of ideas from the lower levels needs encouragement and is essential. The red brick universities of England, land-grant colleges and community colleges of U.S.A., agricultural universities in India were established in response to the peoples' wishes.

The significance of correspondence education

The concept of correspondence education goes well with the concept of life-long education. Education should be available to an individual as and when she/he requires it. This removes the age-old discrimination that people of younger age group alone are ready for higher education. This also removes the time-bound programmes. The universities have to come forward in making this concept alive and vibrant not by formal system alone, but by using alternative channels of non-formal system. The extra-mural departments, the extension lectures and later, the correspondence courses, were the beginnings of non-formal channel. They were started in the 19th century itself but did not come into full bloom until middle of 20th century. Probably, Soviet Russia is the only place where correspondence education was fully utilised from the time of the October Revolution. These course were conducted for adults. A country can progress on all fronts only if adults of the country can meaningfully participate in all aspects of country's activities. Even in 1944, the Sargent Report of British India had recommended that "The role of adult education is to make every possible member of a state an effect and efficient citizen and thus to give reality to the ideal of democracy". In India, so far, the general attitude to adult education has been to view it as connoting adult literacy. The reason is obvious, for the problems in this country is vastly different from what it is in western countries.

> A child must learn to walk before he can run; an adult must be literate before he can hope to derive any benefit from the facilities of education in any wider sense...The main emphasis in the country must, for sometime to come, be on literacy, although from the very beginning, some provision must be made for adult education proper, so that those made literates may have an inducement as well as an opportunity to pursue their studies.

Even when the IEC in 1964-66 studies the problems of education it made a passing references to adult education even though it was felt that adult illiteracy is a hindrance to society and observed.

The function of adult education is to provide

> ever adult citizen with an opportunity for education of the type which he wishes and which he should have for his personal achievement, professional advancement and effective participation in social and political life....An effective programme of adult education in the Indian context should envisage the following-liquidation of literacy-continuing education-correspondence courses.

In India adult illiteracy had been continuously going up and the Government of India launched a large scale national Adult Education programme in October, 78. The efforts in India have to be directed to make the public knowledgeable and thee is need to look at the experiments and innovations made in other countries.

A country like the U.S.S.R. could bring about dramatic changes by launching adult education programmes. Even now correspondence education and part-time education are as popular and as effective as full-time courses. It is seen that thee is no disparity in the standards between the regular and other courses. But the case is no the same in European countries and the U.S.A. The correspondence course were in vogue in U.S.A. from the end of 19th century. The courses never increased their pace. They were considered as an appendage to regular full-time courses and second-rate Premier universities in U.S.A. were giving only lip sympathy and these courses were conducted at a peripheral level and on a small scale.

Special features of correspondence courses

People who frown at correspondence course do not realise that in these courses extra effort has to be put in by the teacher and the pupil. Otherwise it is likely to degenerate into a lifeless course in which the aim is just to score some credits. Dr. Harper who started correspondence course in early 1880s has said that both the teacher and the pupil have to be alive.

> The teacher must be painstaking, patient, sympathetic and alive and the correspondence pupil must be earnest, ambitious, appreciative and likewise alive. The student will either acquire these qualities and succeed or he will remain as he was at the beginning, and fail.

The correspondence course are different, in that there is no peer group and the contact with the main nerve centre (i.e., the university or institute conducting the courses) is minimal. The curriculum here need not necessarily be graded as in formal system and attendance is not obligatory. The formal system is job-oriented and elitism is encouraged. The non-formal system is egalitarian to its approach and gives enrichment to life. The multiple point entry is a great asset of this system. It is less expensive than the regular courses and people can take courses while pursuing their careers/work. The formal system might produce well-qualified people with or without life adjustment.

Non-formal system's objective itself is to take life-adjustment into account. Both systems should be geared to productivity. As far as possible, duplication avoided and innovative methods used. Libraries and resources centres and important regional centres are very essential.

The education in the formal system is largely oriented towards youth. It is generally felt that education is preparatory to life. But in reality, education is continuous with life. The entire population comprising the society should be seen as a natural resources to draw education. Education is nothing but shared experience between teachers and students, a co-operative relationship develops between them and learning becomes a shared experience. The non-formal system takes this aspect into account. This enables us to case out the movement of people in and out of college furthering work-study programmes. The physical and human resources of the school and college facilities would be used to the maximum extent possible. In the developed countries there is a shift towards mass higher learning. In India (as in developing countries) higher education is able to cater to a small percentage of people. But in sheer number the people aspiring for higher education is astronomical. Radical changes are needed in public policies to promote life-long learning like study leave through released time from employment retraining programmes that promise new careers. Here the university has too step-in. It should cease to be a sheltered spot for study and research only. It has to go to the service of the society without over-extending or weakening its position or standards. Continuing education long considered as a second-class function has suddenly taken a new importance, challenging resident education, research and competing vigorously for the resources to carry out its new responsibilities. Continuing education becomes a conduit for the transfer of knowledge from campus to community where it can be applied to solve problems.

The scene in India

In India this type of education assumes greater importance. Education has not yet paid all its dividends bringing in a synthesis and understanding to solve problems in rural and backward areas. In India, the Centre and the states have to spread education for social betterment. Previously education was a state subject but now it has been included in the concurrent list in the Constitution. But it is difficult to say whether the States or Centre could regulate education better. State can look after the regional needs better while the centre can tackle the global changes better. Even in a country like the U.S.A., where private enterprise is encouraged, Federal government is funding several projects towards solution of social problems. Moreover the technological change is running ahead of the ability of social institutions to absorb changes.

To serve the community more efficiently education should shift from elitist to mass education. The school and college become community centres. At the higher level, the university may discover that a programme of continuing education is much less the delivery of an educational service to a given clientele than it is the convening of citizens about critical, societal issues with the process and the impact not the delivery, the aim of highest fidelity. Continuing education about societal issues and citizen participation is among the foremost challenges of the future.

Non-formal education it clear that education is person-oriented and not an institution-oriented. Higher learning can take place in offices, industrial plants, libraries and other centres of community. The community does not remain on the periphery as a client receiving fringe benefits, but it serves as a learning centre. The citizens and institutions participate as advisors in all phases of education and training activity from planning to achievement. At this juncture, universities will make their unique contribution to society at large.

Autonomous institutional model of open education

All these characteristics are necessary for life-long education to flourish. Whether they are sufficient is known from the environment which is provided. The ultimate goal is in its relevance and relation to life problems as those envelop all aspects of a person, being and becoming. The autonomous institutional model of open education for higher education is based on these principles. It has the following features. It is accessible to all including those with no formal qualifications. The teaching, assessment and accreditation functions are integrated-unlike in the external degrees and to a lesser degree in correspondence courses. Thee is no conflict between full-time and part-time students as in conventional universities which run correspondence courses. Hence there is a strong motivation on the part of the institution to experiment with different methods of distance teaching. The institution is free to devise new educational programmes, media methods and target population.

The following are the examples of this type of institutional model:

(1) The Open University, United Kingdom

(2) Allama Iqbal Open University, Pakistan

(3) Athabasca University, Canada

(4) Everyman University, Israel

(5) Sri Lanka Institute of Distance education

(6) Fern Universitat, West Germany

(7) Free University of Iran

(8) Universidad Estal Costa Rica

(9) Nacionel Aleerta, Venezuela

(10) Universidad Nacionel de Education a Distancing, Spain

(11) Centre National de Tele-Enseignement, Paris

(12) University of New England, Armidale

(13) Gakuen Correspondence High School, Tokyo

(14) Macquarie University, Sydney

(15) TV Agriculture High School, Warsaw

(16) All-Union Correspondence Polytechnical Institute, Moscow

(17) Tele-Universitat, Quebec

(18) Memorial University, Newfoundland

(19) Empire State College, New York

(20) Coast-line Community College, California

(21) University of Mid-America

(22) University of South Africa

(23) Central Radio and Television University, China, with 28 provisional TV Universities

(24) Open University, Netherlands

(25) Andhra Pradesh Open University, Hyderabad, India

(26) University of the Air of Japan, (UAJ)

(27) Universities Terluka, Indonesia

(28) Indira Gandhi National Open University, New Delhi, India

(29) and proposed Open Universities in Bangladesh,

Poland, France, Turkey, Nigeria and Palestine (Kaye and Romble, 1981; towards an Open Learning System 1982; Shale 1987)

A chain reaction of establishment of Open Universities all over the world is seen. In India, we have a national Open University and regional Open Universities like in Andhra Pradesh. Already one in Bihar (Nalanda) and another in Rajasthan (Kota) are in the making. The primary role of these Universities in India is to avoid wastage of scarce resources and use innovative an flexible approach to ensure access to one and all and make them cost effective.

Agencies at work

It may not be out of place here to take a look at the functional agencies that are responsible for educational policies in India, the U.K., the U.S.A. and the U.S.S.R. it may be kept in mind, however, that these agencies are an outcome of the political philosophy of these countries. In India and the United Kingdom , the government machinery is in operation with regard to educational policy, i.e., there is Ministry of Education in India and Department of Education and Science (DES) in the United Kingdom. These departments are in overall charge of education and co-ordinates the various educational systems present in the country. Commissions are appointed from time to time to examine the status of education and educational institutions in the country and offer recommendations. Under this comes Radhakrishnan's Report on University Education (1948), Mudaliar's Report on secondary Education (1953) and Kothari's Report on Indian education (1966) in India; Robbins' Report on Higher education and Lord James Report on Teacher Education and Training in 1963 and 1972 respectively, in the United

Kingdom. In the U.S.A. there is no Federal Ministry of Education to set broad educational policy as Education is a state subject. Due to prevailing world trends, in recent times, the federal government is making available special finds...for furthering the education of minorities and for research purposes in sciences. The government also once in a while orders and oppoints committees like report on Higher education during Trumman's time and review committee on Education beyond the High School . But the private foundations like kellog and Carnegie survey the problems of education with the help of leading educationists and exert a lot of influence. The Carnegie's Report on Higher Education is a result of monumental work. The Committee with the help of experts in the field, from the home country and abroad, went into the various aspects of the system of higher education and released periodically reports which have dealt in depth about problems and given recommendations. In the U.S.S.R., the Central Government directed by CPSU is completely incharge of education and gives direction to various institutions. In India and the U.K., there is no guarantee that all the recommendations of the commission have to be implemented. But the reports become the fountain-head from where all the policies emanate. In U.S.A., the recommendations of the reports carry a lot of influence on the policy decisions of various institutions on a purely voluntary basis.

6

Urban and Regional Planning in India and Implications for Planning Education

Though India has had a tradition of town planning and town building since ancient days of Mohanjo-Daro and Harrappa, the evolution of current practice of Urban and regional planning can be traced back to 1898 when Bombay improvement trust was created. During these years, scope of planning practice has widened from piecemeal efforts of road widening, plantation of trees, city beautifying and sanitary improvements to comprehensive planning of cities and preparation of regional plans for integrated development. Planning enabling legislations has been enforced in most of the States, and Town Planning Deportments have been created. One of the major functions of these departments is to organise diagnostic surveys-a survey of social, economic and physical aspects of cities and regions and prepare development plans for the next 20 or 30 years. Planners now have the authority to plan and have been performing the plan-making role in a technical capacity.

However, they do not yet seem to have an authority

to implement these plans. The responsibilities of implementation of these plans are divided and assigned to various agencies, prominent amongst these are the Improvement Trusts, Development Authorities, and Municipalities. But other agencies involved in urban development are a host of special purpose agencies such as housing boards, slum clearance boards transport undertakings, water supply and sewerage undertakings, electricity boards, etc. Similar fragmentation of responsibilities is evident at the State level, where numerous departments under different ministers look after different components of urban development.

We have evolved an arrangement under which town planning departments prepare the plans, Improvement Trusts or Development Authorities or any other agency, created or authorised for the purpose, bear the burnt of the responsibility of implementing the plans. By and large, municipalities are expected to take over developed areas for maintenance.

Improvement Trusts and Development Authorities headed by administrators and, thus, the important phase of plan implementation is not within the jurisdiction of planners.

The Improvement Trusts and Development Authorities perform their functions independent of municipalities; the body of elected representatives. There is also a conflict of interest between these basic agencies. Municipalities complain about Improvement Trusts getting all the remunerative projects and occasionally refuse to pay the share of municipal revenue due to them or take over the assets created by the trusts. Plan implementation suffers as a result of ensuing political bickering.

On the other hand, planners play a technical plan making role, politicians feel left out of the plan-making process and resist implementation of plans in their own areas of jurisdiction. A planning process which does not encourage participation of citizen or their elected representatives should not be expected to make much headway at the plan-implementation stage.

In order to make planning more effective, there is no doubt a need for planners and politicians acting in a joint manner. One may like to suggest that to achieve this, planning departments be made part of municipal administration. But the difficulty lies in the fact that municipal administration has a subordinate status as compared to that to planning departments which is a State-Government function.

Moreover, the low priority accorded to local governments in terms of prestige and pay scales has resulted in poor quality of staff and elected councilors. Metropolitan areas further suffer from fragmentation of urban governments; Calcutta metropolitan District being the worst example with 30 local bodies in an area of about 460 square miles. The situation worsens in the case of metropolitan regions where a host of rural and urban local bodies have to be dealt with and, as is the case of the national Capital Regional (NCR), lying in not one State but several of them.

The need for reform in local urban administration continues to be overlooked inspite of the fact that cities in India are growing at a fast rate.

The Indian Constitution while distributing the responsibilities between the Union Government and the States does not mention urban and regional planning in any of the lists-Union, State and Concurrent.

There is no Ministry of Urban and Regional Affairs in the Central Cabinet and the related matters are looked after by the Ministry of works and Housing.

Urban and Regional Planners do not seem to be taken very seriously by decision-makers in the Central and State Governments.

In essence, urban and regional planners in India have yet to establish their legitimacy to plan, though they have acquired the power to plan. Till now, they have been trying to legitimise their profession on the strength of assumption that planners have a scientific body of knowledge that enables them to challenge irrationality in the piecemeal process resorted to by municipal authorities. Planners have sought to project themselves as independent of political process, and have powers to make autonomous decisions about the future of communities. Present administrative setup gives planning departments such a plan-making role. However, such a set-up has many flaws. As Rein has pointed out that autonomy leads to isolation and independence from political process leads to impotence. Authority which does not have the backing of the political forces and is merely based on technical scientific rationality, offers only authority to propose, but not the power to achieve. The same is now happening on the Indian planning scene. According to latest estimates more than 600 master plans have been prepared for cities and some for regions, but implementation process is not even initiated in most of those cities.

Planning phase to-date in India can be described as that of plan-making without much of planning. Parallel can be cited here with earlier system of planning in North America when Planning Commissions were popular. But

Commission led planning was found to be ineffective, particularly in not seeing plans through the implementation phase. As a result of this criticism, planning was made a municipal function and planners having come closer to decision-makers in the City Halls were able to co-ordinate their activities during implementation phase. However, until the State Governments do something to strengthen the local governments and improve their status, planning staff will remain reluctant to serve as a part of municipal administration.

The efforts of planning national economy have given wide ranging powers to central governments over States in urban and regional development programmes. In a vast country like India where each State represents a micro-nation with its own culture and language, a centrally directed planning effort is not suited. Under such a system, public participation is minimal and demand on administrative resources very high. Thus in the interest of administrative efficiency, political accountability and public participation, it is essential that planning administration be radically reorganised. State governments should be given more powers to bring about such a reorganisation within their own political framework, and urban administration be streamlined and given adequate powers and resources to deal in a co-ordinated and forceful manner with the intricate problems of modern cities and their regions.

However, the reorganisation of the administrative system relating to planning is one step towards rationalisation of planning framework in India. The immense gap between the available financial resources and the scale of investment needed for urgently required urban and regional infrastructure, is the other problem basic to all problems. Here are needed and making plans and programmes which are compatible with these resources. One of the criticisms of planning efforts in India has been that planners have prepared plans without much regard to fiscal and administrative resources of governments responsible for their implementation. Also, these plans are prepared as an exercise in urban design without much concern for existing priorities and constraints on resources. This is a reflection of the fact that an overwhelming majority of our planners come from civil engineering or architecture background. Most of the planning schools in India restrict entry of students with social science background. The Institute of Town Planners, India, hesitates to recognise planning courses with less of design content.

The leading planners and teachers in India today were trained in then heavily design oriented planning schools in Britain and the United States of America. While the planners in those countries are moving away from the heavy physical planning orientation they had, to a planning framework involving society's goals and value systems, planners here seek to prepetuate the planning methodology which has not proved useful.

Weaknesses of comprehensive planning have now become quite apparent. Planners had promoted the concept of comprehensive planning as a result of lessons learned from piecemeal planning. They had understood that solutions of problems without a comprehensive plan usually resulted in worsening of other problems or simply shifting the problems to other locations. Thus, comprehensive planning was presented as an approach of problem solving with the knowledge of all inter-related factors and within the time perspective of changes affecting them. The concept got crystalised in the shape of a comprehensive development plan; in case of towns and cities, a plan of proposed land uses accompanied by transportation plan and municipal services plan, and in the case of regions location plan of settlements with potential for growth and proposals for improving physical linkages and distribution of facilities and services. Not that planners have not been aware of social and economic dimensions of their profession but somehow our pre-occupation has been with physical dimension.

Basic points criticising comprehensive planning were raised by Altshuler. He asserts that comprehensive planners' claims to comprehensiveness, if they are to be persuasive, must refer primarily to a special knowledge of public interest. In other words, a comprehensive planner should be able to identify the unified public interest and express them in terms of community goals. There are difficulties here, since different interest groups may have different goals which are competitive and conflicting. Some means of bargaining process through public participation is suggested in identifying the public interest. But, problems of finding discussants and proceedings for meaningful participation by a public which would represent all shades of interest groups have been raised. Some other weaknesses of comprehensive development plans have been pointed out by Friedman Candeub, Gans, and others, They point out that comprehensive plans are:

1. Static; once-for-all statement about the future shape of cities or regions 20 or 30 years hence.
2. Makework Plans; filling gaps through intuitive judgement.
3. Demanding in terms of co-ordination which never

exists; co-ordination is more an exhortation rather a reality.

4. Not even comprehensive; as they are confined to physical aspect.
5. Ignore poor and weaker sections of society; are suited to business community interests and other middle and upper income class residents.
6. Focussed on long-range problems which is often at the cost of immediate needing immediate attention.
7. Time consuming; by the time are prepared are outdated.
8. Generally not backed by statements of fiscal institutional measures or policies.

It seems quite obvious from what is said above that master plan type of planning being practiced today is narrow in outlook, rigid in approach and difficult to implement. Planning schools which prepare their students for this very type of plan making role, not only help perpetuate these flaws in our planning approach, but also face the danger of getting inflicted and stifled by the rigidities and unrealities inherent in the approach.

In view of the lessons learned from the experience of planning in the past, elements of the kind of discipline we ought to pursue in future are being states below.

1. Planning as a Process: formulation of strategies and tactical schemes with clearly defined goals, careful selection of options, choosing amongst alternatives, continuous evaluation and revision.
2. Participatory Democracy: encouraging public participation.

3. Positive Planning: clearly delineated objectives and action oriented plans rather than remedial or negative policies.
4. Pluralistic: if about 80 percent of our population lives in rural areas and a large majority of our total population is poor, our planning effort should also contain a similar bias towards rural areas and the poor.

Thus, if we need to be flexible, realistic, and incorporate values and goals of society, we need to substantially increase the non-physical content of our planning approach to impart creditability to what we propose for physical improvement or development. Inevitably, what we want to change in the process of planning must get initiated in our planning schools. If our students have to be prepared for a change seeking role, and the change we need to bring about in planning profession to make it more realistic, the structure of planning education has to be so devised that it becomes the hallmark of flexibility and reality.

Fagin and Gans have projected thesis that planning is basically a methodology that is transferable to all efforts to achieve selected goals by systematic application of resources in programmed quantities and time sequences designed to alter projected trends and redirect them towards established objectives. This approach argues that what makes planning a discipline and its practice a profession is what it does and how it does not where and to what it does. According to them planner should be an expert on delineating action programmes to achieve chosen whether it is applied to manpower planning, open space planning, mental health services planning, or chalking out development programmes at urban, regional or national level.

Fagin has further identified the elements of a planning discipline-planning per se, not the traditional planning which tries to compartmentalise planning into city planning, regional planning, transportation planning, etc. The elements are;

1. Analysis; division of whole into component parts (system into sub-systems), understanding of how these components function and how they interrelate with each other.
2. Synthesis; assembling of parts into a whole to create new constellation of ideas, arrangements and programmes. This element is partly creative and partly helped by analysis.
3. Collaboration; with specialists, planners in different agencies, and different interest groups.
4. Education; education about planning within the ranks of profession and outside.
5. Mediation; balancing different interest groups. Planners' input here is to indicate possible actions, taking into consideration various constraints and possibilities, implications of each action.
6. Prediction; predict possibilities and implications; use of simulation, statistical, probability methods, etc. are suggested here.
7. Advocacy; advocacy of different interest groups.
8. Administration; spelling out plans in terms of actions, monitoring of implementation, legislation for action, identification of agencies involved and assignment of tasks.

If we accept the thesis that a common theme of planning runs through planning efforts in various substantive areas, then the planning education in these substantive areas can be provided through a single programme designed around a common core. The above elements identified by Fagin can be very helpful in developing a broad based core programme in planning education. The choice of substantive areas would depend on various factors such as areas of specialisation of available faculty, financial resources, etc. But, as far as possible, the issues and problems at national, state or local levels should determine the choice of the substantive areas Areas such as Rural Planning and development, City and Metropolitan Planning, and Planning for the Poor come readily to our mind. others pertaining to a region can be picked-up by the planning school located in the region.

There are many variations in structuring of programmes of planning education to take care of orientations in specific areas. Seelig has identified five such alternatives: (a) mandatory programme with little or no choice of elective courses (b) mandatory core programme plus choice of streams (c) mandatory core programme and electives (d) streams without mandatory core (e) no mandatory core and no streams. Seelig's work is based on the study of North American planning schools conducted in 1971. According to him a mandatory programme with little or no choice of electives is rarely offered now. Alternative (b) has the advantage of providing expertise in a specific field of study and is offered at many leading planning schools. The disadvantage of alternative is that many students pursue a programme which has no strong emphasis on a specific area related to urban problems and they often find it very difficult to relate their educational experiences to their future careers. Alternative (d) was offered only at the Massachusetts Institute of Technology (M.I.T) and was considered as one of the best programmes available there and possibly even today. however, this structuring of the programme there had become possible because of a strong faculty with strong commitment to specific streams and access to courses offered in nearby Harward and Boston Universities. Lately, M.I.T. has gone back to the alternative (b) as it is felt that a core consisting of set of courses focusing on quantitative methods is essential. The skill in the use of quantitative methodologies is considered essential for planners as decision-makers seem to want the proposals backed by hard facts. The alternative (e) was, then, unique to the University of California at Berkeley. According to Seelig, many professionals and educators considered Berkeley's programme the best one available. Major reasons for the success of the programme was the school's large and diverse faculty and the fact that many of the faculty members were among the most capable professionals and educators available then.

An analysis of programmes available in seven of the eight planning schools (Ahmedabad School excluded) in India indicated that alternative (a) is adopted with some variation. The School of Planning and Architecture, new Delhi, offers three streams in urban and regional planning, housing and community planning and traffic and transportation planning after a common core programme. However, once a stream is chosen, all the courses offered under the stream have to be taken. Choice of electives within a stream is not available. Kharagpur School provides two separate specialisations, one in city planning and the other in regional planning with a small common core. Roorkee School has chalked out a revised programme to be effective from 1978-79. Under this programme choice of electives is proposed to be substantially increase. However, this School offers one core programme with no strems. An overwhelmingly large majority of students in most of the schools in India come from architecture and civil engineering background. Few with Geography are also admitted. The entry of students from other disciplines (with the exception of Ahmedabad School) is limited by the schools.

Conclusions

Urban and Regional Planning as practiced to-date is characterised by lot of plan-making without much of planning. Planners in India have succeeded in achieving power to plan but not the power to implement. The marked failure in being able to get plans implemented may result from many sources. The institutional framework within which plans are prepared and sought to be implemented has so developed that plan-making task has become independent of political decision-making task. Planners are equipped to play a technical plan-making role but not the political persuasive role of getting the decision-makers realise the strengths in the plan so meticulously prepared. The practice of planning the way it has developed visualises plan implementation as a stage different from plan-making rather than as a process under which feedback from plan-implementation is very much part of planning. The plans are strong in physical and design aspects but not tied to hard issues of resources availability, resources mobilisation and plan administration.

Planning schools prepare the students for this very plan-making role which the planners in India have been playing for well over two decades now. If we have to focus our attention on plan-implementation, education programmes may have to be provided with depth in various aspects of plan-implementation. For this, planning education may have to be broadened in scope so as to supplement the present heavy emphasis on physical aspects by introducing courses on capital programming, budgeting, public financing and plan-administration. Students may have to be exposed to political decision-making process by frequent visits to the meetings in local government institutions and development agencies. May be, a course on political behavior analysis is desired.

One of the skills on which planners have to draw upon heavily, to convince decision-makers about the soundness of the plans, is the ability to use quantitative methdologies for identifying problems, exploring alternatives, and suggesting options. One of the ways in which we can hope to achieve better plan-implementation is to provided the plans the backing of the hard facts of a planning situation. Thus, planning education programme may focus on a set of core courses in quantitative methods.

One of the implications of what has been said immediately above is to move away from a generalist planning framework of planning education to one which provides for expertise knowledge in the problem areas requiring immediate attention in the context of our national, regional and local situations. Some of the substantive planning areas identified are rural planning and development, planning for the poor, and city and metropolitan planning. Some of the important sub-areas are mass—transportation, rural housing, low cost urban housing, urban government and plan administration, public finance etc.

It is suggested that various planning schools in India should attempt to structure their programmes around a set of core course on quantitative methods, plan-design, capital programming and budgeting, political behavior and plan-administration.

Around this core, depending upon faculty specialisation available, various streams providing opportunity of specialisation in one field or other may be attempted. However, in the context of the present composition of faculty in our planning schools such a restructuring of programmes can be achieved only in the long-run. In the short run, we should attempt to increase the number of electives and encourage a diverse faculty with expertise in atleast one of the various dimensions of planning activity.

However, in order to equip our planning schools with such a diverse faculty in the long tun, we may have to immediately discontinue the present practice of favouring architects, engineers and to a certain extent geographers only for admissions in planning schools. We may have to identify a range of disciplines which might contribute to planning and encourage students from all these disciplines.

7

Emergence of Non-formal Education in Developing Countries

NFE has been described as an international movement. The purpose of this chapter is to illustrate NFE, noting the three perspectives of NFE as a system, a setting and a process in developing nations. Examples will be drawn from Asia, Africa, the Pacific and the America to illustrate the global nature of the NFE phenomenon. These examples will range from the consideration of national systems programs to single programs with limited objectives and specific audiences. Five national systems and five individual programs are discussed.

National examples

Jamaica

This Caribbean nation is a small Island of significant geopolitical importance. In history has witnessed several important stages, including a period when slavery was a major fact of the economic and social life of the island.

As far as terminology is concerned, probably because of Jamaica's links with Britain, the terms 'adult education' and 'non-formal education' are used interchangeably.

Two significant aspects of adult and non-formal education in Jamaica are that they are viewed as being central to the twin objectives of development and nation-building. There are many types of education included under the adult and non-formal education heading which is given below:

1. Fundamental adult education: that which provides the basic ideas, skills, and techniques for modern living. This includes literacy, family, and remedial education.

2. Vocational education for out-of-school youths: that which provides non-formal education outside the regular school system for young adults.

3. Formal adult education: that which parallels the state examination system primarily designed for children.

4. Liberal adult education: that which is concerned with the pursuit of knowledge for its own sake and for individual self-fulfillment. This includes cultural education and educative work of the media.

5. Citizenship education: that which provides specific public education for adult citizens outside traditional formal institutions.

6. Rural adult education: that which is primarily intended to upgrade the quality of education of inhabitants of rural communities, mainly farmers.

7. Health education: that which is designed to improve the health practices of Jamaican citizens.

8. Consumer and savings education: that which seeks to improve the knowledge and sophistication of the buying public, and to increase its propensity to accumulate surpluses and to spend judiciously.

9. Business, industrial and commercial education: that which provides in-service industrial and business training for members of the Jamaican work force.

10. Co-operative education: that which prepares interested individuals to participate in and manage co-operative enterprises.

11. University adult education: that which is provided by the Department of Extra-Mural Studies of the University of the West Indies and includes remedial education outside the regular school system for young adults.

The lists indicates the breadth of provision in terms of purpose, provider and client group. The provision is designed to include all citizens: the range of activities covers social, civic, cultural, vocational and economic aspects of development: even the University of the West Indies is included as a significant provider for people not normally considered as its students.

A key issue for NFE and nation-building has been the dual-culture nature of the nation. Jamaica was a colony and 'white' values, including the English language, predominated, even after political independence. The influence of white values has been challenged as part of the NFE process. Creole has been seen as an alternative to English and black cultural values and traditions, which originated in Africa from hence the original slaves were transported, have been emphasised. In this respect music, dance and traditional crafts have received attention in NFE programs and been valued as important in the nation-building process. This attention to music and dance has potential for developing a significant indigenous 'setting' for the NFE program. NFE is Jamaica has been able to address the significant problem of the two cultures, and point to further development recognising the two cultures and their relevant strengths, and their potential in this development.

A number of specific programs in Jamaica illustrate the way NFE seeks to contribute to nation-building and development. In literacy, the Jamaican Movement for the Advancement of Literacy (JAMAL) came into existence in 1974 and has become an integral part of the Education Ministry, indicating an acknowledgment that the problem is going to continue. Progress and experience in dealing with the problem of literacy have resulted in attention being devoted to the provision of suitable materials for neo-literates and for the training of personnel involved as literacy tutors. For those who have achieved literacy levels, personnel involved as literacy tutors. For those who have achieved literacy levels, programs are offered in the fields of business and co-operatives, and for management in the public and private sectors. In a recent commentary on the Caribbean literacy experience, Jules noted two lessons from JAMAL. Firstly that JAMAL was not "an isolated educational undertaking...the first step...in an ongoing process that sought to establish education as a permanent right from the cradle to the grave" and secondly "the successful conduct of literacy work on a national scale requires the overcoming of the traditional and sectarian divisions which characterise our social relations."

As far as culture is concerned, the Jamaica Festival Commission was established in 1968. In addition to specific festival activities, the Commission has unearthed material and performers to maintain the develop interest in the popular culture. With regard to social and community development activities, the Social Development Commission has been significant with youth services, community centres and rural land settlement.

A major problem for even small nations such as Jamaica is that of co-ordination of NFE activities. With such a vast range of programs and many providers, the management problem is one of ensuring that all programs contribute to the goals of development and nation-building.

Thailand

Thailand is a unique Asian nation. The country did not become a colony of one of the European powers during the imperialism era. The three dominant features of Thai social and political life ar Buddhism, the Monarchy and the army. The Buddhist religion has had, and continues to have, a significant influence on that lives of the vast majority of the population. The Monarchy is held in very high esteem in the nation and provides a strong unifying focus for the nation. The army has played a leading role in the political history of modern Thailand. The balance maintained between these three major influences in Thailand provides a degree of stability and unity of a type not often reached in developing nations.

As far as NFE is concerned, there is a National Commission on Non-formal Education that co-ordinates activities throughout the nation. Although there is a special Department of Non-formal Education as a separate entity within the Ministry of Education, it is recognised that other agencies contribute to the national NFE effort. In official documents twenty one government departments and instrumentalities, from the Religious Affairs Department and Fisheries Department to the Supreme

Command Headquarters, as well as thirty NGOs and commercial organisations, are recognised as NFE providers.

Non-formal education is recognised in the national plans. NFE has been delegated responsibility for ten areas in the Five Year Non-formal Education Development Plan 1987-1991.

1. eradicate illiteracy among the work force, provide compulsory education to out-of-school children and youths and promote further education opportunities for the out-of-school population;
2. expand news and information system through establishment of reading centers very village, public libraries in every district and learning resource centers, and utilize mass media for education more effectively;
3. expand and improve vocational training activities with an emphasis on closer linkages to the demands of the labour market and local learning opportunitiers, greater collaboration with private commercial sectors in training and the promotion of self-employment;
4. integrate efforts to foster moral and cultural development in all types of non-formal educational programmes;
5. develop for target groups with special needs and problems particularly those with different ethnic and linguistic backgrounds, the handicapped, the prisoners and other disadvantaged groups;
6. create close integration and linkages between formal and non-formal education to provide life-long learning opportunities;

7. improve quality of non-formal education through research, development, training activities and the establishment of data system for planning at national and provincial levels;
8. elicit greater involvement from the community, educational institutions, religious organizations and the private sector in organizing services for the out-of-school population;
9. decentralize planning and administration of non-formal education to operational levels and promote greater participation of target group representatives in program organization and evaluation; and
10. improve coordination and collaboration among agencies involved in non-formal education.

As far as the NFE Department is concerned, administration is carried through provincial, district and sub-district operations. The Department also developed regional offices whose role was not to become involved in the line management of the Department but rather to act as service centres for program development and specialise in areas of provision or advice, for example in the development of special materials or to develop distance education methods and strategies.

The rationale of the Department's work within the Five Year Plan has three major emphases: basic education, news and information, and skills training. Basic education, which is also called Education to Provide a Foundation for Living, includes literacy training and particularly resources for the neo-literate. The second emphasis is facilitated because the Department is responsible for libraries. An important Departmental initiative has been the setting up of Village Reading Centres, designed as resources for non-literates and neo-literates as well as locations for the print and other materials from government and non-government agencies related to health and agriculture for example. The reading Centres are simple structures that are built in traditional styles and with traditional materials so as to form a natural part of the village. A recent article indicated that a train library had been set up in train carriages near Bankok in a railway workers' residential area. The train library was also designed to be a natural part of that setting.

The area of skills development being the Department face to face with the problem as to the degree to which NFE becomes the foundation of vocational training. The Development appears to be following the policy of providing skills training courses as the demand develops but also encouraging other providers to offer programs so that the Department is not relied upon as the sole provider of skills training for all levels of skill in all technical and vocational areas.

A special feature of Thai NFE has been the development of a specific theoretical approach to learning, called Khit-pen. The Khit-pen man is one who is a problem solver. The approach reflects a combination of Buddhist philosophy and some of the principles of Western adult education. Khit-pen provides more than a setting for Thai NFE. It also contributes to the process of NFE is the country. The three emphases of the Department reflect the three types of knowledge required by the Khit-pen man to become a successful problem solver. In a book on Khite-pen, Nopakun explains what the Khit-pen man can do:

"A man who mastered the process of Hit-pen will be able to approach problems in his daily life systematically. He will be able to examine the causes of his problems. He will be able to gather the widest range of information on possible courses of action and weight the merits of each option, based on his own values, his own capabilities his personal situation, and the degree of each solution.

Two important special programs promoted by the Thai NFE Department have confused on a special target group, and a methodology. In the hills of Northern Thailand lives a group of people with a culture quite different from the majority of Thais. A special program, called the Hill Tribes Project has been carried out over a number of years to cater for the special needs of the Hill Tribes and their distinctive culture and social organisation. The Radio Correspondence Project on the other hand his been designed to cater for the needs of young persons who have left school and are working, usually on the family farm plot, and yet wish to continue their education or catch up on missed schooling. Use is made the written word with correspondence materials sent out to students. These materials are supplemented with radio broadcasts which go to air times suitable for the workers. In addition, meetings of groups of student are held with tutors.

The flexibility and progressive approach of the Thai NFE Department is illustrated in the following example. Concern expressed that there were urban groups for whom the Department should be providing educational opportunities, as well as rural Thais. One such group is the 'bar' girls who provide services, especially for tourists, in the many bars in Bangkok. The decision was made to provide opportunities for the girls to participate in specially designed programs to that the girls, if they close, have the opportunity of finding alternative employment and different life. However, the decision was also made that a non-government agency (NGO) may be more successful with such a program and the program delivery was negotiated with such an agency.

Thai NFE provides a good example of a changing policy and administration to accommodate the changing needs of society. Thailand's Khit-pen also illustrates an indigenous process in NFE where the emphasis is directly towards the individual, as it is the individual who is to become the problem-solver.

Indonesia

Indonesia is an archipelago and one of the most populous nations on earth. Yet its population is not evenly spread over its many islands and while Java is one of the most densely populated areas in the world, there are many uninhabited islands which are either un-inhabited as Kalimantan, or not densely populated. Indonesia was once a Dutch colony and achieved its independence only after an armed struggled. The new nation was multi-lingual and multi-culporal and thus was faced by a lack of political unity. A response to the divergent linguistic situation was the introduction of a national language, Bahasa Indonesia. To establish political unity a set of national principles, called Pancasila, was promulgated. The principles are:

Goals and objectives

PENMAS has been given the following goals by the government:

- Thrust on basic attitudes and skills for development
- Education for social leadership

- Cultivation of good reading habits
- Education for women
- Education and mobilization of youth for community welfare.

These specific goals are in support of the government's primary objective: to improve the quality life of the Indonesian people under a system governed by the national philosophy.

- *Belief in god almighty*
- *Humanitarianism:* all people of the world are related in one large family; there should be humane treatment of all human being.
- *Nationalism:* all the different ethnic groups of Indonesia are now one people; there should be unity and love of the nation-state.
- *Democracy:* all citizens should practice mutual self-help and consensus-building discussion.
- *Social justice:* there should be adequate food, shelter, work, and opportunities for all.

The national principles and national language have had implications for Indonesian NFE.

NFE has generally been the responsibility of the government and the general principles have been set out in the National Plans, for example in the Fourth Five Year Plan, the NFE brief was:

a) The reduction of illiteracy through the formal and non-formal systems;

b) increasing labour force productivity and opportunities for self-employment; and

c) providing a common language for the diverse ethnic groups in the country.

The administration of NFE has been attended to by a unit within the national Education Ministry. The Indonesian approach to NFE has been to coin phrases to represent the programs, for example PENMAS and more recently DIKMAS, derived from the title of the Directorate of Community Education - Pendidikan Masyarakat. The Dikmas program is administered through the various levels of government, the national, provincial, district and sub-district.

In operational terms, there are two major NFE programs, both associated with the word 'kejar', formed from the worlds 'bekerja' meaning to work, 'belajar' to learn. The two programs are Kejar Paket A and Kejar Usasha Paket A is the literacy program, developed in Bahasa Indonesia. It consists of one hundred graded books or readers and covers a range of topics concerned with issues of living and working in Indonesia.

With the help of a tutor, the participants i.e. out-of-school youth, older adults, mothers, work through the Paket A readers. Supplementary readers, usually devoted to local subjects of interest, have been developed particularly by the provincial level of Dikmas administration.

The second type of program, Kejar Usaha, is concerned with income generation. A village group can be granted capital to develop an industry or service. Support is provided by Dikmas personnel and other government departments and the capital is not refunded to the government but can be used to develop further commercial activities. Kejar Usaha groups that have been quite successful and concerned with such diverse activities are catering, sweet making, small scale silver trinket making, special cane basket making to hold a specific amount of rice and suitable for carrying on the head, and making road gravel from volcanic deposits in the river. Usaha projects frequently result in a renewed interest in Paket A. In the basket making program, the success of the activity resulted in an additional project being supported to collect the appropriate raw materials and take the finished products to distant markets.

A central consideration in the Kejar programs is mutual assistance. Volunteers are used extensively in Paket A program as tutors. The support in Kejar Usaha is for groups, not for individuals, and the desired outcome is for the Usaha group to support other groups in the village. The emphasis on the group does not however reduce the importance of the individual response and responsibility in and for Kejar programs.

Australia

Australia is included in this list of national NFE portraits because NFE has been described as a world-wide phenomenon and although Australia can be described as a developed nation, it is also developing, is in the Asia-Pacific region, has been a colony and has to achieve its independence. Some of the factors important currently in Australia may become important or should be considered as possible options for developing nations.

Australia does not have a national plan, nor a Bill of Rights, nor a system of NFE. It does have a constitution and is a federal nation with two levels of government, namely national and state. Normally, there are no real mechanisms to coordinate NFE-type activities and there are no specific goals set for NFE-type activities. However, two general goals are discernible: as Australia is comparatively new national and consists of migrants from many nations. The concept of nationbuilding is important: as dependence on the export of primary products and raw materials changes and as manufacturing and service industries are viewed as significant for economic development, education, and that includes the non-formal sector, will increasingly be judged according to the degree to which they contribute to the nation-building and economic development objectives of the national government.

A very significant factor in recent thinking about non-formal education, or adult and/or continuing education as it is normally termed, has been the publication of a piece of research, entitled "A Nation of Learners". The survey showed that 60 percent of adults had participated in an adult education activity in recent years. Such a high level of participation was unexpected and exceeds earlier figures. The statistics have lifted the profile of NFE in Australia.

Although increasing numbers of young people are staying to complete full secondary education, i.e. 12 years of schooling, there are still high levels of illiteracy. Not only are there failed products of the school system but the numbers are swelled by migrants who are not literate in English as well as numbers of the indigenous people, the Aborigines. Adult literacy is being tackled s a national problem and a variety of government and voluntary agency program using different approaches, individual tutoring, classes, the mass media and computer technology are used.

In vocational education is the primary provider has been the Department of Technical and Further Education (TAFE). This department has trained the trades persons and technicians. The higher education system has trained the professional occupations. All provider in vocational education are paying close attention to the vocational demands created by new technology, people changing jobs and women re-entering the work-force. A special form of vocational education with a long and high standing has been agricultural extension which provides an educational and advisory service for the many fields of primary industry that have been so significant to the national economy.

Special programs of a non-formal nature have been developed, by governments for the so-called 'disadvantaged' groups, such as Aborigines, migrants, women, people with physical or mental disabilities and the isolated. In contrast to these programs, the tendency for adult and continuing education has been for the 'user-pay' principle to operate so that participants pay for their adult and continuing education. In this climate, there has been a growth of commercial providers who compete with government agencies and a variety of non-government agencies, many long established, for learners. A strong entrepreneurial spirit has been created in Australian adult and continuing education in the whole range of providers. For example, recent changes in higher education institutions have resulted in them forced to concentrate on continuing education programs, and clients for their programs, who can afford relatively high fees to cover a wide range of costs and even generate profits.

Changes that the national government has initiated to higher education have resulted in developments significant for Australia's version of non-formal education. One change has witnessed the breaking down of the barriers between credit and non-credit programs, i.e. those for which a certificate, diploma or degree is awarded and those for which such an award is not gained. A false dichotomy has thus been removed. Further, the distinction between vocational and non-vocational education and training has been blurred. Associated with this has been broadening of the concept of training to move beyond the notion of training being very specific to skills that may be immediately applied and being focused on a limited range of relevant technical skills. Personal and inter-personal skills, as well as more long range technical skills, are now being accepted as an integral part of vocational training.

Such a brief description of some aspects of Australia's style of NFE does indicate the sorts of directions NFE in a developing nation may move but also raises questions about creating barriers between different forms of education and of placing narrow definitions on other forms. For example, the question can be raised as to what definition is given in a country like Pakistan to vocational education and whether it is short term or long term in its projection of the value of that training? Again, what prospects are there for NGOs providers of NFE in countries such as Pakistan? Or what role is entrepreneurial NFE likely to play? Will the commercial providers emerge outside NFE the system or will the system be so planned and organised and commercial providers can be viewed as having a legitimate role within a broadly conceived system of Pakistan NFE?

Papua new guienea

Non-formal education in this new nation in the Pacific will

be considered from the point of view of a broad historical sweep.

In pre-colonial days, education was a village concern, associated with the ongoing activities of the village. The instruction or teaching was carried out for the young. The concentration was on the young because they could, it was assumed, learn all they needed to know for full adult life and participation in the village's life. Instruction for the boys was by men and for the girls by women.

As a consequence of colonial rule by the Germans or Australians, village-based instruction was replaced by the formal system of the school. Education was provided in varying degrees to selective groups within the indigenous population. The system, and particularly the examination system, was based on models taken directly from the colonial nation.

Thus when PNG gamed independence in 1975, the new nation was faced with many problems. In educational terms there were two related questions: How could education foster the nation's development, and what sort of education should this be? and How can the problems created by the existing formal system be overcome?

The following rationale emerged as a role for NFE. It was viewed as being the most important means for meeting the educational needs of all the people, particularly in relation to literacy, if and when the problem was seriously tackled. Secondly, NFE was also viewed as being a potentially powerful tool for national development, particularly rural development.

But the formal system had prestige and NFE was considered second-rate and the NFE system of education was cheap as it received only 2 percent of the education budget. The dilemma for the people, as well as for governments, is illustrated in the following example. In the colonial period 1965, the December results of the Grade 6 examination indicated that only three out of 26 candidates had passed. There was trauma in the village. While there was rejoicing in three households, what of the order 23? What about the aspirations of the students, the parents, younger children? What of their attitudes towards formal education? Village support for the school declined. The incident occurred in 1965: independence took place in 1975. However, the formal system had been largely left intact.

Certainly in the later colonial period and the independence period NFE provision has extended. From this inception with the work of missionaries, a wide range of providers has developed - provincial authorities, village-based organisations, government departments, volunteer groups, NGOs and overseas development aid agencies. Co-ordination of programs has been lacking and many overseas-inspired projects have been short-lived.

There is NFE activity, there have been policy developments relating to NFE, there have been views expressed about the potential role of NFE in the nation's development. Before NFE can become an effective instrument, however, there needs to be more political will and with it the allocation of resources. There also needs to be a clear identification of national goals and the co-ordinated use of NFE, and a reformed formal educational system, to achieve general development objectives and specific social and economic objectives. In those circumstances NFE may be a more effective tool for the development of the people and the nation.

Program examples

National literacy campaign in zimbabwe

There have been three stages of the Zimbabwean revolution: independence that was achieved in 1980; economic independence that is gradually being achieved; the emancipation of the mind.

The removal of illiteracy was conceived as a major part of the third stage of the revolution. 2.5 millions of the population of 7.5 million were illiterate in the newly independent nation. Prime Minister Mugabe, in launching the Literacy Campaign in July 1983, asserted that the people could not really have freedom and that the mind could not really be liberated while they were not literate.

The campaign was well planned. Advice was gained from Tanzania where a similar program has been successfully conducted. The setting appeared to be appropriate as the mobilisation to remove illiteracy was linked in time with the demobilisation associated with the end of military hostilities that had been associated with the gaining of independence. The campaign was a national mobilization. Involvement was gained from the central government to the village and included the private sector. There were District Literacy Co-ordinators as well as a large pool of Voluntary Literacy Teachers.

The original goals of the campaign were ambitious. One million illiterates were to be reached and enrolled and made literate by 1986-87. Performance has not matched the goals. By 1984, 117,461 people had been enrolled, in a ratio of six women to one man. By 1986, however, the enrollment figure had dropped to 82,138 with a ratio of five to one in favour of women. Clearly the national objective could not be achieved.

Why was this so? In evaluation projects associated with the campaign some important developments were isolated. For example, men in the campaign were interested not so much in functional reading material but more academic material so that they could enter the formal economy. Also, the high ratio of women enrolling had resulted in the belief that the campaign had lost its momentum and needed revitalisation. Alternatively more limited objectives could be set and adjustments could be made in the light of feed-back and evaluation.

There was, however, been another reason offered for the lack of success for the campaign. According to his schema that relates political ideology to literacy activity, there had been a change in the ideology in Zimbabwe from the revolutionary to the reformist.

The campaign can be revived and revitalised. It is difficult to discern whether the original objectives are attainable. A campaign, in contrast to what he describes as a project or program, is still possible. Its success will depend on leadership from the 'top' and a commitment to the revolutionary principles and processes that were associated with the original mobilization. The problem for the leadership will be in integrating the revolutionary aspects of the literacy campaign with questions of whether a full scale campaign that is going to lead a change in the status of women is consistent with the socialist/capitalist mixed economy that is being developed and whether the men of the villages will be content with a new generation of literate women. The Zimbabwean experience indicates the many important implications of a major literacy campaign.

Bhola also comments that a literacy campaign is only

possible in revolutionary situation. Bureaucracy and inter-departmental co-ordination are only capable of organising some sort of project or program. The description of the Nicaraguan literacy 'crusade' provides a useful comparison with the situation described in Zimbabwe and, in addition, an example of options in Bhola's schema.

Training roadside mechanics in nigeria

Roadside mechanics make an important contribution to the economic life of developing nations and transport becomes more significant and bicycle become motorcycles and horsedrawn and become trucks. As an area of vocational training does the apprenticeship system have relevance to mechanics in this situation, does it work and, if so, how? Who are the apprentices, and the trainers? What levels if literacy are appropriate?

Oduaran has made a study of the apprenticeship system for roadside mechanics in the Nigerian city of Benin. The report is not a description of the program but rather a study of some features of the program.

Oduaran found that the majority of the apprentices were in the 16-20 age group. But there were older people serving as apprentices. There are important implications from the age spread, not only in terms of the experiences of the apprentices but also the fact that being a mechanic must, in the eyes of young and older apprentices, have career prospects. Two thirds of the apprentices were illiterate according to national tests of literacy and their own admissions. the important questions arising from this figure are how they cope with the training, how much better literacy skills would contribute to their ability to be effective apprentice learners and how set levels of literacy may prove to be a somewhat irrelevant barrier to the entry of young men into the apprenticeship.

The apprentices themselves only suggested that literacy may have helped their progress and specifically thought that labeled pictures of some of the parts of engines may be useful. The apprentices seemed to cope, to continue successfully through the program. Many of those who left early before finishing the course seemed to be able to find employment as mechanics. The notion of requiring a certain literacy level at his moment would seem to be educationally desirable but, in fact, likely to restrict opportunities.

The reason for the lack of pressure on literacy levels for apprentices is related to the fact that 45 percent of the trainers of the apprentices are not literate either. The trainers are very conversant with engines, have in some cases been trainers for a number of years and are adept at the oral communication and demonstration that is the central teaching technique for apprentice training. The communication mechanism is Nigerian pidgin English. A reason for the use of this medium is that apprentices come from a number of tribes of the country with different 'first' languages.

So the apprenticeship system operates in a non-literate ethos, for the majority of those training and being trained. No evidence was presented that the system of mechanical repairs was inefficient. At that time the requirement for literacy levels for entrants or trainers would have caused serious disruption to the mechanical repair operations in the city. Planning of requirements for levels of education for entry into occupations or for literacy levels needs to be based on a study of the existing systems in operation, the personnel involved and their backgrounds, the teaching and learning methods used and the costs and timing involved in any proposed changes.

Requiring higher levels of general education for entry into occupations may be viewed as a step in the modernization of a nation. However, the question is not simple. Research has shown that there are particular types of literacy and illiteracy associated with apprenticeship training such as in the vehicle maintenance industry and that improvements in efficiency may not necessarily be achieved with a simple raising of general educational entry standards. Further, where are effective trainers to be found and new training techniques developed?

Rural development in south korea

In the 1960s there was a strong drive for industralisation in South Korea. The drive was successful but as a consequence a gap appeared between the urban rich and poverty in rural areas. Under the initiative of the President in 1971, the Saemual Undong program was launched with Saemaul Education as a major instrument for the movement. The Movement's aims were threefold:

"First it seeks to modernize Korean society on the basis of its socio-cultural traditions, aimed at not only material improvements but also spiritual enlightenment. Secondly, it is directed toward improvement of living standards for individuals, communities and the whole nation. Thirdly, it is a movement towards spiritual reforms led by the government to establish new values and human relations congenial to national development."

It was a national program with strong support from the President and the national bureaucracy. But there was also scope for initiatives from individual villages and many successful activities were promoted in this way. The initial phase of program was the issuing of 35,000 rural villages in 1971 with 335 sacks of cement and rods of reinforcing steel for construction and maintenance of local roads and bridges. The Movement has grown so that there are now four phases: urban, rural, factories and schools and many Ministries are involved - Culture, Fisheries and Agriculture, Health and Social Affairs and many non-government agencies.

The intensity of the focus has resulted in virtually all NGOs in rural development being closely associated with the Movement and its educational function.

One of the process problems in the development of Saemaul was the lack of local leadership, from village leaders to government officials. Training Institutes were thus set up, initially at the national level and then locally. BY 1979, 40,000 people had passed through the national institute. Having followed the program, they took their newly acquired knowledge and skill back to their villages. The three emphasis of Saemaul training were: based the training on real experiences, and particularly successful models; accentuating doing rather than talking; self-evaluation and development through discussion. 85 other institutes for training were established - 49 by government and 36 by non-government agencies.

Saemaul Education worked through the Saemaul Village Centres, prompting educational activities related to development and organisations, for example for women or a library.

Saemaul was successful, as was Saemaul Education. In macro-economic terms, the earnings of farmers increased over six-fold in the 1970s. Model villages, that had accepted the spirit of Saemaul, were identified and became focal points on interest nation-wide and for overseas visitors. Identifying reasons for the success of such ventures is complex. One possible reason, important in an examination of NFE, is perhaps the fact that the Movement was "indigenous to Korea in method and style".

Health education in India

This ease study emphasises the methodology of a health education program in India. The program was identified that the dietician-trained health educators were having little impact on the health of the villages. It was as though there was a need to establish a bridge between the two worlds of the villagers on one hand and the health educators on the other. The writers' response to this communication gap was the analogy. They argue that an analogy is like a plough that can prepare a population's field of associations for the planting of a new idea, in their case, relating to health and diet. The preparation work in this context was as important as the seed, in this case the health idea. The writers approached the religious leaders, indigenous medical practitioners, astrologers and politicians to gain insights into language use and thought patterns. As a result of these explorations in language and health, they were ready to proceed on the seven steps in forming appropriate analogies. The writers also provide two examples of the end-product of the seven step process. The second relates to assisting pregnant women adjust their diets during their pregnancies.

"I would to make a connection between the growing rice paddy field and the growing child. The paddy plant is like a child. The paddy plants needed in the field are like the baby's needs in a mother's belly. When planting a paddy field one needs to do this with good feelings, with happiness and proper preparation, if a good crop is to grow. Like that, during pregnancy a woman needs to have good feelings and a happy home environment. The seed bed is like a woman's family environment. One must care for the field, the seed bed, not only the developing plant, to have a good crop. If the field is not given proper treatment and enough fertilizer, then the rice plant does not develop or germinate properly. In the same way, if a mother does not receive enough food to be strong and have good blood, the illness mandama dosa develops."

Analogical Framework: The following analogy was offered to the villages:

Stages of Development	*Sinhala Term*	*Human Development Counterpart*
seed	bitteravee	see
germinated seed with root	vela vee	fertilized seed in uterus
rice plant	gayam phalleh	pregnant woman
flowering plan	bandi (bandiya also denotes 'big belly')	pregnant woman in her last trimeter

Drawing upon the above analogical framework, a discussion ensured of vitamin/mineral supplements and immunization."

The understanding of subtle aspects of local language use, in this case in the area of analogies, may prove the differences between success and failure in a NFE program.

Regional development in China

The final example of a program is drawn from China and illustrates the role of the Chinese variation of NFE in regional economic development. The special economic zone of Shenzen is on the coast near Hong Kong and was opened up in 1980. There has been a significant growth in population as well as changes in economic and social conditions.

Because the emphasis has been on a re-orientation of economic activity, the major target group has been the worker, and thus worker education. The program has been designed to provide educational services at various levels, of various standards, in various form, and through various education channels. The areas covered in the programs included: electronics, micro-wave communication technology, micro-computers, interior decoration, finance and banking, tourism, hotel management, marketing and fashion design. Such an extensive program involved both formal and non-formal sectors but was primarily concerned with an 'adult' audience.

It has been claimed that the "Shenzen achievements in adult education are not only remarkable from a quantitative but also a qualitative point of view" The Shenzen program is a very good example of the marshalling a wide range of educational resources to achieve economic development and change.

8

Promotion of Non-formal Education through Technology

What is technology? For many people technology means computers and satellites, lasers and heart-lung machines. In the context of a discussion of NFE, technology is defined as those devices and equipment designed to assist learning. In other words, technology is just a form of teaching aid. Goals are set for learning: methods are selected to assist in achieving those goals or as aids in reaching the goals. Technology offers a range of methods to assist in the achievement of learning goals. In other contexts at other times, the term technology may not have been used and a term such as 'audio-visual' aids used instead. The present definition of technology may appear to be far removed from the bytes of computers or the dazzling complexities of satellites but the definition provides a means of incorporating ail forms of technology within a single discussion. If the discussion was related to agriculture, then the definition would have indicated that technology was a means of assisting agricultural production.

What the definition also highlights is that technology is not just what is called 'high tech' or 'high technology,' the powerful computers and intricate lasers. There is another, and sometimes overlooked, area sometimes disparagingly referred to as 'low tech'. In educational terms the distinction is between computer-assisted learning and the chalkboard. If the discussion was concerned with agriculture, then the automatic header would be high tech and the low tech.

Let it be clearly stated at the outset of this chapter that the authors are convinced that the problems of NFE are NOT going to be solved by technology, and certainly not by 'high tech'. Technology, both of the high and law types has a very important role to play in assisting NFE, for technology is a method for learning, to achieve its goals but alone it has not the power to achieve these goals, as sometimes enthusiasts believe. What is required is some sort of balance. In the Consultants' Report, two programs were dealt with in detail - one using television, the other using face-to-face teaching. Such recommendations and planning represent the sort of balance being advocated. The chapter is not anti-technology or anti-high technology. What is needed is calculated judgment.

Attitudes towards technology

The American adult education academic Jerold Apps in a Foreword to a volume a microcomputers and adult learning noted three positions taken by adult educators to the whole range of new technology. The first was that the educator has become aware of the new technology but had not quite decided what to make of it. The second was that after examination of the technology the educator had decided it had no application to adult education, while the third referred to the educator who had become excited about the technology and wanted to incorporate its use into every aspect of adult education. The second position is dangerous for NFE: the third is potentially dangerous: the first is also a problem for the educator may take too long to make up his or her mind. What is necessary is some overall understanding of technology as it relates to NFE and a means of helping those concerned make a decision. One final question needs to be addressed before the remainder of the chapter deals with satisfying the two requirements noted in the previous sentence.

Why use technology?

The educator and the learner want to be successful in their educational activities. Methods that will assist in the process, then, are likely to be used, if known. Technology, as noted above, provides some of these methods. The particular contribution of technology is that it assists learning by appealing to the human senses, sight, hearing and touch. As learning centrally involves a physiological process, it is argued that making an appeal to one or more of the senses increases the potential for learning or the speed of learning, or even the enjoyment or excitement of learning. The appeal to the senses was a foundation for the use of the term 'audio-visual'.

Classifying technology

Various means have been suggested for classifying the various types of technology used as aids in the educational process, from the discussion by Pula to that of Romiszowski to those of Heidt and Johnson. A composite scheme, drawn from these and other writers, is set out below to describe as complete as possible the range of technologies appropriate for use as learning aids in education. The scheme consists of five categories, essentially exclusive but allowing for the use of several aids from different categories, if the educational purpose is thus served. Because the concern is learning, categories are developed according to the senses upon which the various technologies rely. So the categorisation is based on the senses of seeing, hearing and touch. The other major term used in the categorisation is projected. Projection consists of using light in some form to create an image or picture, still or moving. The five categories are listed and some examples of the technologies associated with each category are noted and discussed.

1. *Visual/non-project:* This category contains a large number of items. The aids rely on their visual impact without the aid of projection. A very important item in this category is the printed word: books, newspapers, journals, periodicals and newsletters, the favourite means for networks and NGOs. As Stewart has stressed, newspapers are a 'forgotten medium for adult education'. Further, newspapers, either the large distribution dailies or cheaply made local news sheets, are a valuable and relevant reading resource for neo-literates. The category also includes a wide range of boards on which to write or draw illustrations such as the chalk or white board. There are newer types of this style of aid on which you can write in a marking pen and then have a single photocopy of the material written on the board. Then there are flipcharts, white paper held together and written upon and then either discarded or filpped over so that another sheet can be used. This first category includes photographs, photocopies and prints, charts, graphs or posters.

Combinations of media can be used so that pictures can be placed on a felt board to help narrate a story or illustrate a problem. There is some scope with some of these items to involve the sense of touch. Participants can place the felt pictures on the board or they can be encouraged to handle the materials or re-locate parts of the village model in different places. However, the emphasis is on the visual sense frequently as an aid to the spoken voice.

2. *Visual projected:* These items require some form of projection and therefore power in the form of electricity or batteries. Items in this category include a range of what are commonly called 'transparencies'. These may be in the form of a long film called a strip film because it can be wound through the projector backwards and forwards to allow the learners to see the material on each frame of film. There are also slides, i.e. individual film transparencies. There are normally projected one at a time but there are projectors that allow them to be shown rapidly one after the other because the individual slides are housed in a cartridge or carousel. The device called the overhead projector allows the instructor to present material prepared on thin sheets of transparent material to a group. The nature of the overhead projector is such that complex overheads can be prepared using overlays to illustrate complex ideas and systems. A great deal of information can be miniaturised and stored in micro-film. A special micro-film reader enlarges the small print so that is easily read by the naked eye. Usually only one to three people can read such material at one time unless another form of projection is also used.

3. *Audio:* This category appeals essentially to the sense of hearing. Items in this category include radio, vinyl records, tapes, the compact disc, language laboratories and the telephone. Radio can be thought of as a mass medium broadcasting to large numbers over vast distances. However, the development of small and efficient transmitters has resulted in radio becoming a much more localised medium so that local and regional communities can have access to the medium not only as listeners but as broadcasters and presenters. The nature of recordings has changed from the large and easily broken recordings of the 1940s to the compact disc of the 1980s. The large tape recorder of the 1950s has largely been replaced by small cassette players. The storage of cassettes is also easier than reel tapes or even large vinyl recordings. The language laboratory consists of a number of tape recorder-type outlets set up in individual booths with headphones, and a central control panel as is demonstrated from the diagram.

The individual learner in the booth is able to follow the taped instruction, and sometimes provide oral feed-back, while the person at the central control can monitor the individual booths. The name language laboratory has been used because the item has been extensively used in the teaching of foreign languages. The telephone is not only a medium for one to one communication. By using a telephone with an attached speaker-microphone one person can talk in a two-way discussion with a group. An extension of this is to have a group of people in scattered locations linked together through the telephone system so that they can communicate with each other. Such a process is called a teleconference. Not all telephone systems, particularly in developing nations, have the technical sophistication to carry the teleconference operation. The teleconference has been extensively developed in Australia and a useful reference on the use and operations of the technique is by Lundin.

4. *Visual projected with audio:* In this category, the audience can see as well as hear. In this category are included the various sorts of movie film, television transmission, and video-recordings. Television in its transmitted form was well established in Western nations before the advent of video-recorder. In some developing countries the video-recorder has arrived in many locations before broadcast television. Efficient and comparatively cheap television transmitters may provide the opportunity, as with radio, of more locally produced and operated broadcast television. An interesting combination of two items mentioned above illustrates this category. The tape-slide presentation combines the audio of the tape with the visual of the projected slide. Special techniques have been developed to make the automatic movement of the slides synchronise with the sounds of the tape recording. Items in this category are at the 'high tech' end of the spectrum of aids for teaching/learning. Some of the refinements of the above items include closed-circuit television (CCTV) by which an educational program can be produced in one part of a building and shown in another part. It is television with limited transmission. Also, the item teleconferencing, noted in 3 above, can be conducted using visuals and voice and is called video-teleconferencing. Such a process is also called 'interactive' because those involved in the various

locations can interact with one another. The transmission of such video-teleconferencing has been facilitated, as has normal television and voice transmission, but the use of satellites. However, such techniques can also be carried out through terrestrial communication technology.

5. *Manual:* At a simple level, this category includes such devices as sewing machines and typewriters. And the recent items in this category are based on the 'key board'. As a result of developments in what is called the behaviorist approach to learning, B.F. Skinner was instrumental in having teaching machines developed in the United States. These were machines before which learners performed specified tasks in the prescribed way and received an indication from the machine that they had successfully completed the task or were given additional work to do so that they could succeed. The micro-chip has resulted in the teaching machines becoming museum pieces. The computer has been used to develop a whole range of teaching programs. As the learner sits at the keyboard and manually operates the computer in performing tasks, the computer indicates the level of success, whether the learner can proceed to further instruction or whether remedial exercises have been diagnosed. Two frequently used terms in computer learner are computer assisted learning (CAL) and computer manager learning (CML).

So as to provide a balance and to avoid getting lost in high tech, it is important to note that there have been other 'touch' technological aids, for example blocks and marbles, and of course Cuisenaire rods. One of the oldest of these aids is the abacus, and there is its modern counterpart needing batteries the calculator.

They have been significant developments linking the computer with satellites to educational institutions, other learners or resource centres. There are endless possibilities of linking various form of technological aids and methods. At the level of high tech Johnston has called some of the newest methods of bringing separate items of technology together to form new methods as 'hybrid' media. However, hybrid media can be developed throughout the range of technology. In Chapter on Target Groups mention was made of persons with disabilities. For older adults who have lost their sight 'talking books' and talking newspapers' have been developed by putting the written texts of newspapers and books on cassette tape for the blind people to 'read'. Whereas the five categories provide a basis for gathering together the wide range of technological learning aids, the categories are not exclusive and combinations of methods from different categories may provide the required method for a specific purpose with a group of learners.

The previous section has made a quick traverse of some of the wide range of techniques to which the term 'technology' can be applied. The purpose of the section was to give broad overview, and understanding, of the scope of technology applied to learning. The next section seeks to help NFE educators ask the appropriate questions so that the correct choices are made in the section of what technology to use for NFE programming.

Choosing the appropriate technology

The term 'appropriate technology' has come into common use, particularly to emphasis the full range of technology available and avoid the magnetic attraction of technology at the high tech end of the spectrum.

There are many ways proposed to assist administrators, programmers, and tutors decide which the range of media to use for a program or a particular teaching session. The simple answer is what will achieve the best result, or what it is alleged will provide the best result. However, it is suggested here that a number of questions should be seriously addressed by whoever is responsible, administrator, programmer or tutor.

But, as suggested, there have been other ways advised to help the educator decide. Some suggest the 'best use' for particular technologies. However, this is a very simplistic approach. There are too many factors to consider in teaching/learning situation to be satisfied with a best use criterion. Another method is to provide a checklist on which various key factors can be 'ticked' to give an overall rating of the effectiveness of a particular piece of technology. Such checklists can include questions for tickling such as "Is the equipment available? Has the equipment been checked? Is the learning group experienced with this peace of technology? The problem with checklists is that if they are to be effective, they have to contain a long list of questions, some of which may be totally inappropriate for a particular technology or learning situation. Also, it is very easy to tick a particular item, rather than carefully consider a tick is the correct response. Sanchez has written about his list of 'do's and don'ts' when he is personally involved in preparing his own technology - usually of the non-projected visual category. While his personal list, because it is developed from his own experience, is not likely to be of great value to others, the idea of such a personal list has some value.

Two more sophisticated methods are suggested by Heidt. One method, also advocated by other writers, provides a list of advantages and disadvantages of a particular methodology.

The advantages/disadvantages method has some usefulness but lacks relevance to specific cultural settings or with special groups of learners. It may be useful for individual educators to develop their own advantages/disadvantages list with various technologies in various settings.

The four questions

1. What is the cost? It is suggested that NFE planners and personnel need to be conscious of the cots of NFE programming. Note was also made of such approaches as cost-benefit and cost-effectiveness. The area of the use of technology to support learning is a very useful area to apply these principles because on the one hand some technology is very expensive and on the other there is continuing question of the choice between a range of alternatives. What are the comparative costs, for example, of developing a set of videos or a set of photographs or board figures for a felt board to support a nutrition-improvement program? Then other questions, as to how many need to be produced, how will they be distributed and at what cost, what will be the costs of substitute or replacement materials and will there be location costs involved in their use, will require costing. These can be calculated. Then the assumptions have to be made about how many people can be reached with the various methods being investigated and the final, the really difficult question, to be answered on the basis,

preferably of evaluations of previous uses of the methods, is how effective the various methods are likely to be. Then the costs are related to effectiveness and a decision made on which method. This can appear a simple approach. There are, however, difficulties. There frequently significant indirect costs. They may include hidden 'subsidies' such as the cost of transport or of studio time or of the un-charged for work time of staff. In areas of technology, there are also what is known as 'infra-structure' costs, for example making certain that the telephone system can carry the required teleconference calls or that there is sufficient power for projector generation.

It was not co-incidental that the Consultants' Report on the 1987 UNICEF NFE Conference included a media-delivered program. The costings are discussed in more detail in Chapter 18. The important point to note here is that the costings were attempted and included. In an otherwise very interesting report of a Seminar on the Role of Television for the National Literacy Campaign Project in Thailand no mention is made of costs, except that in a footnote on pages 39-40 it is reported that ASPBAE provided financial assistance in 1986 and will continue the assistance in 1987. This sort of oversight should not be continually accepted by NFE administrators and programmers whether the medium being used in television or flip-chart paper.

2. What are the cultural implications? The cultural dimension of NFE, and learning, have been stressed. Therefore, the cultural implications of the use of technology as an aid to learning in NFE need to be carefully considered. It is not adequate to apply the sorts of 'best use', 'advantages/disadvantages'

approaches developed in Western nations to other cultural settings. The significance of the 'cultural' dimension in the use of technology of various types will be illustrated from four studies.

Akhila Gosh has shown how women in particular areas of India just do not understand, or misunderstand, many of the films that have been prepared by the government to encourage them to change their behaviour for example in family planning. The women's reactions were associated with the fact that they could not 'trust' the women in the films, or that the women in the film were disgusting because they were publicly talking about matters that were not discussed in that open manner. Technically very useful films were culturally inappropriate, and possible counter-productive' for the educational program they were designed to support. The cultural factor must be recognised.

There are also significant questions about the nature of the culture's views on knowledge. The studies indicate the importance of knowledge, both in relation to science and what? Ogunniyi sought to understand the level of scientific thinking in relation to selected natural phenomena among a group of illiterate adults in Ibadan, Nigeria. As might be expected superstition and non-scientific ideas were used to explain the natural phenomena. Technology based on 'correct' Western concepts of science would be completely misunderstood by these Nigerians. Conversely, technology that was based on their superstitious ideas may have some impact in helping them understand Western science. In a longer article, Colorado has explored the scientific ideas of the North American Indian. They do have a science and it does have laws and standards; it is just that these are different from those of traditional Western science. She suggests that there should be a 'bridging' of the two types of science. If science is a basis for knowledge and knowledge is central in the development of technology to aid learning, then the developers of the technology, and the users, need to be conscious of likely differences, defined by culture, in the understanding and defining of knowledge, and science.

There is also the question of 'technology transfer', that is taking some piece of technology, developed in one culture, and using it in another. The agricultural system was referred to in the introduction. In this context, the notion of technology transfer may refer to the introduction of tractors developed for Western agriculture into the farming systems of Africa or Asia. Musa has vividly described some of the disastrous effects of dependence caused in developing nations by the importing of technology. In relation to technology and education, de Vries has examined the question of technology transfer with regard to the introduction to computers to teach numeracy to adults in the African city of Soweto. The details of the case study are interesting, but his conclusion is most relevant here. "My conclusion may sound obvious, but it needs to be said: one should not accept without question that the same arrangements apply in Third World environments as in the First World. Great care should be taken to determine whether the new environment has the necessary infrastructure to accommodate the innovation before it is introduced". Mausa highlighted the effects of technology transfer: de Vries has called for close examination of infrastructure. Conboy and D'Cruz have also called for an examination of effects. That examined the impact of distance education methods on rural and isolated groups in developed and developing nations. In discussing not the immediate impact but the longer term, broader impact, they questioned whether the technology used was not having a detrimental second order consequence on rural identity and local community culture. What then are the impacts of the transfer of technology from one culture to another on the existing infrastructure and significant aspects of the local culture? The NFE educator cannot avoid responsibility in this regard by claiming "I did not know". Such an excuse is no longer acceptable.

So that a completely negative picture is not produced, the final study in this section reports a successful program, and one that was culturally appropriate. Barker, White and Taylor report how computer managed learning was used in an Australian higher education institution as a means of achieving an organisation development goal. This 'new' technique using new technology was used, with new work group and patterns, to move the institution to a new phase in its development. In that setting, although there naturally some teething problems with the program, the program was culturally appropriate - one possible reason for its success.

As these case studies have indicated, the cultural dimension of the use of technology in education cannot be overlooked.

3. What is the role of the learner? In the Heidt Media Capabilities Matrix, there is a column for student response. As a general question, frequently overlooked, the educator should ask what the learners will be doing while the technology is being used. Will they be entirely passive watching various sorts of

visual projected technology? Is this desirable? The educator can occupy large groups of people with visual projected technology with sound but are they learning? Is there an opportunity for the learners to discuss the issues being presented or to ask questions - it is difficult to ask questions to a person appearing on transmitted television.

The importance of learning in the use of technology has resulted in modifications being sometimes made to the technology. For example, because movie films are often long and do not provide the opportunity for those watching to talk about the content of the movie, there developed trigger films. There were short films that posed an issue, usually dramatically. Then the film was stopped and the audience discussed the issue in groups, frequently suggesting 'what would happen next'. Then the film was re-commenced and 'a' particular solution or version of what might happen was played out on the screen and after the movie was complete the audience were able to discuss the movie interpretation in relation to the scenarios they had developed.

Having a clear priority for the sorts of activities in which the learners will be involved results usually in a variety of technology being used. Mahai discusses two programs, in health and nutrition in Tanzania. The programs appear to have been successful. One of the reasons would appear to be that in the programs, in which a variety of technology was used including ration and print, there was the consideration given to the activities of the learners, especially in relation to the overall objectives of the program.

There is a danger in the use of technology in learning that the learners may be just entertained or that so much technology is provided that there is no active learning planned for the learners.

4. What are the professional implications? Having the equipment is one area of concern, having people who can work the equipment, and attend to breakdowns, is another question, frequently overlooked. These technology-literate people may not be part of the NFE system, but from wherever they are obtained, they need to be present and at the ready. In the Learning Centres of the Consultants' Report, their is a need to have local people 'trained' the level where they can deal with the technology needed, e.g. the monitors for the television programs. As far as the NFE staff are concerned, there is needed to be technology literate But what that really means is unclear as the more general question of what general literacy means. They should know how to operate and make running repairs to the equipment. Such knowledge is not gained in a one-off learning experience. Technology changes. If personnel are to be given a full or partial responsibility in relation to technology, it is vital that opportunities be given for them to upgrade their knowledge and skills and the technology, particularly if it is high tech, becomes more sophisticated. If technological specialists are employed, then it should be expected that their knowledge, as with all specialists, will, or should, become sop specialised that the other non-specialists in the organisation will not understand what they are understanding. The development of a specialisation in just one aspects of technology, namely computers, in adult education has been evidenced by the appearance of a new journal "International Journal of Computers in Adult

Education and Training". The people who use, and maintain, the technology are as important as the technology itself, perhaps more important. An interesting illustration of technology may be seen below.

9

Some Developments in the Workers Educational Association

It seems appropriate to open this look at where we are going, and what we are going, particularly in the last decade, with words of R.H. Tawney. Those heady days of the Rochdale Guild where Tawney, the doyen of adult education, set the seal on the tutorial class are an inspiration to us and surprisingly relevant to the pattern we have developed in the last ten years. That Branch of the WEA an a full programme which included lectures, reading circles, Saturday evening lectures, art gallery and museum work and excursions.

Rochdale is famous in WEA history not only as the home of that pioneer tutorial class taken by Tawney but also for having responded to 'the interests of the 120 members of the Carters and Lorrymens Union who requested and attended a class on "The Care of the Horse" Similar matching of provision to a wide range of needs preoccupies the association today in its concern to bring the resources of education to bear on the interests and demands of the people. Greater recognition of the individuality of education is beginning to emerge, thankfully reinforced by these early examples, and involvement in practical areas is seen as inevitable if the education provided is to be appropriate and relevant. Lord Ritchie-Calder's contribution to this volume reminds us of the indivisibility of our society and that our educational needs must span science, technology and the arts.

Changes in society have clearly had a repercussion on the WEA not only in terms of its type of provision and experiment but internally in terms of its own development. More than other providers, the WEA is involved in a two-way process and, as a student democracy, reflects the turnmoils of society at large. There are tensions between different sections of the voluntary body, and sometimes between professional and voluntary body, and sometimes between professional and voluntary worker, but these are often creative in outcome and ensure an awareness which leads to relevance in provision. This uniquely British organization operates on shoe-string budgets, without its own accommodating for courses and with only a minimum of basic audio-visual aids. It has survived for practically eighty years because of its capacity to respond and be flexible — to provide educational fare of relevance to current issues while yet remaining independent of involvement. This independence is something particularly precious and important to maintain against any suggestion that the State might take over the work. Many voluntary agencies, it is true, have fulfilled their function and handed over, but there is a special need, in any libertarian democracy, for an agency to preserve the right for full and balanced examination of political, religious and ethical subjects with freedom from direct local or national government control. Apart from this question of democratic independence, however, there appears to be such a vast remedial educational job to be tackled that the role of a voluntary agency with adult student participants is unlikely to complete its task in the 'eighties.

Concern for democratic participation and for the reduction of educational inequalities has strongly influenced our recent innovative work. At the beginning of the decade we were just getting to grips with our first experiment in 'community education' as it is now understood, although the WEA has, of course, always been most closely involved with the community and its branches are very much of the local communities to which they belong. Perhaps we have been laying the foundations for rising to the challenges to which Ritchie-Calder draws our attention. The most amazing thing is that so much innovative work has been attempted with such limited resources and in a period of continually increasing financial cuts and crises.

One of the most encouraging breakthroughs in reaching people whose problems were not only educational but in many cases stemmed from extreme social deprivation, was an experiment in action/research in which a WEA Tutor Organizer was attached to the Liverpool Educational Priority Area Project for three years The case for such a post in the inner city area, to work with local communities free from the demand made on traditional tutor organizer posts covering wide geographical areas, was made to the DES and accepted. Tom Lovett, the first holder of the post, has written an account of this work which included many new initiatives in community education. Considerable interest was sown in the project by the Russell Committee and as a result the need has been recognized to develop new forms of provision. Since those days many others have extended the community education role as distinct from community development, and many tutor organizers now have some part of their work in this sphere.

Although the full range of these community education activities cannot be detailed here, it may be of interest to show these examples of the sort of work undertaken:

- acting as co-ordinator in setting up a scheme of volunteer tutors for adults with reading or numeracy difficulties and of other schemes of individual teaching and of learning exchanges;
- scripting and producing programmes for local radio and television, some for use by listening or viewing groups, and involvement of adult students in programme production as an educational process;
- helping people to set up and contribute to a community newspaper;
- building up a group, over a period of time, at a day centre for the unemployed;
- acting in a counselling and advisory role—sometimes as an essential preliminary to establishing credibility and presenting a viable education programme;
- attending meetings of community associations and tenants' groups in what is often the equivalent of a teaching role;
- working with parents to promote the home/school relationship so vital to the child;
- acting as a non-directional resource person to groups, ready to provide information and counseling on specific educational aims;

- disseminating information digests in everyday language for lay people and community groups, setting up study groups, and arranging follow-up conferences and the presentation of formal evidence the representations to the politicians.

Another innovation has been in the development of Family Holiday Schools, first stated in 1968 at Glynllifon College near Caernarvon where children were looked after while their parents studied, and later expanded in association with Leisure Plan at Pontin's Holiday Camp at Prestatyn into a full programme of educational, sporting and recreational activities.

The development has steadily grown and study groups have also been offered at holiday camps in the south. It is encouraging that campers have responded to these 'taster' opportunities and each year more people opted to attend the WEA study groups. Last year over 500 people 'signed up' to study in this way during one week in the Prestatyn camp alone.

The realization of so much untapped potential involved a formidable amount of planning. It has involved provision for up to 2,000 adults and 2,000 children spread over a range of nearly sixty activities and afforded an exciting glimpse into the possibilities of adult education right across the boundaries of Responsible Bodies and local education authorities. A tutor of a group studying British political parties reported on the enthusiasm typified by a man who had left school early and had subsequently never participated in any organized educational activity. When asked to write an account of the main ideas in an election manifesto, adding his own critical comments, he told the tutor: 'the way I see it, it's a challenge, so I'm doing without my after-dinner pint to get on with it.'

Stemming from pioneer work by WEA tutors in Blackburn on trade union studies for immigrants, which included the production of a teaching pack, a project was set up known as TUBE. This project has been funded with a five-year grant through Manchester Education Department. Activities have included running courses for ethnic minority communities in Manchester as well as weekend and day schools. Work is also undertaken to give white people an increased understanding of ethnic minority groups and to combat racism in places of work.

An example of flexibility and swiftness of response to political policies was in Liverpool where the WEA enabled some twenty community and voluntary groups to make responses by 11 March 1977 to the Secretary of State for the Environment on the Inner Areas Study Summary Report, although publication data of the document give only two months for a reply. Through the Community Development Officer of the City Council, community groups were offered publicity material overprinted with details of meetings; a set of information sheets summarizing the main points of the Report, together with some reactions to it, was prepared by university staff; and the WEA organized courses for those who wished to study the situation. Financial support and help in producing all this was given by Liverpool Council for Voluntary Service. Some twenty groups met and mandated delegates were then invited to a day conference on 5 March and reports were collated to produce a collective viewpoint. This conference elected an editorial board of eight persons who produced a report *In Our Liverpool Home* and this was presented to the Secretary of State.

Collaboration with BBC Radio Merseyside developed

from a fairly traditional series of adult education programmes to an experiment in community involvement with a series called *Living Today*. Topics included 'The family', 'The neighborhood', 'The school', 'The Church', 'The local authority', and 'National government in relation to local problem's. Classes were held in community centres and pubs. Various other series were subsequently undertaken which led to stimulating interest and acquaintance with adult education among a new audience. A phone-in programme in collaboration with the university and the LEA just prior to launching the main winter offering of courses, proved most successful.

The Second Chance to Learn course, which was initiated by Liverpool University Institute of Extension Studies and is now increasingly part of the WEA responsibility, is a good example of a joint University/WEA collaboration particularly in the early stage of pump priming. Funded initially by a Job Creation scheme and then for a period by the Joseph Rowntree Charitable Trust, its finance now comes through the Inner City Partnership Scheme. The course is one day a week with intensive tutorial back-up for people how lift school at the minimum leaving age. There is no formal entry requirement and nursery facilities are provided for students with young children. Designed to help people face the problems of inner city Liverpool, particularly the problems of housing, welfare, race and unemployment, the course includes consideration of government economic and social policies, and the impact of these on life in Liverpool, as well as problems of law and order. The course covers Liverpool's history from the viewpoint of the working people with exploration of the oral and visual record through the use of tape recorders and cameras. A writers' workshop complements the history workshop and students are encouraged to continue further study in more traditional forms through colleges and universities. Special links have been developed with the Northern College which has a 'link tutor' partly based in Liverpool.

A significant piece of collaboration with the Open University was an action/research attempt to identify the learning problems of the early school leaver in relation to Open University study. This project funded by a Social Science Research Council grant was planned after a number of experiments with course material from the OU Foundation Course in Social Science in various contexts such as in a new torn, in a government training centre and in a number of factories and on a course for police officers.

For the final project four groups were set up, one in a factory, one of students from the inner city areas of Liverpool, one a group of apprentices and one a group of students in lower grades of the Civil Services. The outcome of the year's work, where students studied material from the Open University foundation course 'Understanding Society' course units, enabled an evaluation of factors which included the techniques of tutors, the written material in the course units, the use of audio/visual aids and the learning attitudes of students. Interest was shown by the national press and interviews were given on *Look North* national television. An industrial shop floor worker is worth quoting from a BBC TV transcript dealing with the research...in production engineering or anything in production, where you are on a conveyer belt system, where your brain isn't allowed to function really, you're a machine while you're at work and when you call upon you brain to start functioning and using itself it just doesn't turn on because of what, eight to ten hours a day, your brain is actually doing.'

It reaffirmed what we have long known in the WEA, that working class adult students possess a fund a talent and intelligence which has not been developed in school. Early school living has deprived them of the chance of developing their potential, though perhaps this is not foremost importance if the concept of the system of continuing education becomes a reality in our post-industrial society. Lord Cohen, when launching our Jubilee Appeal Fund at Liverpool University, recalled attending a WEA class before the First World War and said 'Whereas at school I was told what to think, at the WEA I was shown how to think.' Admittedly many of the students involved in the project were self-selected volunteers and their responses to a test designed to estimate breadth of general knowledge revealed a standard equivalent to the average sixth-form school leaver.

Suggesting stemming from this research were:

1. that the Open University should pursue a policy of 'positive' open access with a deliberate attempt to recruit students from traditionally disadvantaged sectors of society;
2. that the Responsible Bodies and the Open University should be encouraged to launch experimental schemes to stimulate interest among shop floor factory groups;
3. that the Open University and the WEA should endeavour in a number of appropriate areas to move away from traditional areas of study location and base themselves in industrial premises;

4. that the Open University should allocate a number of guaranteed places to industrial concerns willing to co-operate in a joint scheme.

Having learned many of the difficulties in mounting such projects were also hoped that more extensive research would be pursued recognizing the limitations of this initial exercise. The full report of this study is entitled *Given Half a Chance*.

The WEA is still pursuing it avowed purpose of expressing the needs of workers for adult education. We shall continue to develop workers' and trade union education in our own provision and also represent their views and requirements to other providers, especially the universities.

The expansion in our programme of Trade Union Education mainly with the TUC has been a major development. This work now represents approximately forty per cent of the West Lancashire and Cheshire District provision. With around 1,000 day release places per year, courses have involved many of the leading activists in the city. A WEA Industrial Branch on Merseyside enables local trade unionists to identify their own needs and run their own educational programme and to respond quickly to local and national current issues. Educational day schools and week-end schools are arranged for specially requested topics such as the one on microprocessors which attracted over seventy people. The activity largely centres on instilling confidence in shop stewards to cope with the increasingly complex legislation and to equip them with the skills they need in dealing with often highly controversial issues. Health and Safety courses have increasingly featured in this provision and help was given in setting up a Merseyside Hazards Group. The range of issues and areas covered draws on the disciplines of economics, law, politics, biology, chemistry and industrial relations, and the application of these to work experiences promote the best of adult education, ensuring that academies have their feet on the ground and bring liberal studies to bear on problems faced by activists.

In an address to a WEA National Conference on Arts and Working People, Jack Jones saw the increase in leisure as a challenge to the trade union movement. It was clear that there was a need to bring the Arts into the workplace and the unions should regard this as a matter for negotiation with employers along with other conditions of employment. It is equally clear that paid educational leave for the wage earner has to be developed in this country. Despite the great advance of the International Labour Organization in 1974 putting the responsibility on constituent governments to pass legislation giving workers a statutory right to PEL, no draft legislation has yet been considered by the British Government. In Europe a number of countries are moving in this direction and in North America steps are under way towards implementation of PEL. Otto Feinstein of Wayne State University has pioneered an impressive programme in the United States - the University Studies and Weekend College programme for auto workers and the unemployed in Detroit. This course was run in collaboration with the United Auto Workers Union which participated in drafting courses and recruiting. In Italy PEL arrangements for the 150 hours course have benefited over 450,000 workers in the first four years, and now extend throughout industry to about eight million workers. Most workers are entitled to 250 hours PEL. the TUC has asked for action on the

ILO convention, but there has been no strong pressure from either trade unions or adult education bodies to press on with this most vital and important development.

The autonomous nature of all WEA Districts inevitably leads to differing patterns of provision so it is somewhat surprising to find a considerable degree of similarity in their range of provision and staffing between the two neighbouring Districts in the north-west which have little or no formal contact. The variety and range of provision includes rural areas, from the villages of the southern Lake District to the Cheshire plains, and urban branches running their own programmes in most of the towns between. Work in the new towns like Runcorn, Warrington, Kirkby and Skelmersdale has been experimental, often in community centres, with provision ranging from courses on the pre-school child to preparation for retirement. alongside providing traditional courses, the WEA is essentially flexible and responsive to local initiative. Voluntary workers often play a part in initiating and helping to run experimental courses such as 'Breaktime' in Chester - a series of meetings led by a tutor but allowing a programme to evolve from the interests of the participants. Mothers on new town estate in Runcorn attend while their children are cared for in a playgroup.

In Liverpool itself, a recent venture in collaboration with Liverpool Education Authority has been the provision of courses of spastics. These stemmed from a week-end school on gemology, pottery, music and politics. In collaboration with Liverpool Adult Literacy Centre courses have been mounted at an intermediate level to help in the transition to taking up further study. There is an interesting parallel to the early Rochdale Guild's pressure for classes to be provided on composition and arithmetic in the class held on two afternoons a week for policemen and postmen with an average attendance of thirty. This brings to mind the course held for policemen in Liverpool around the Open University 'Understanding Society' course units, and the WEA has made a similar contribution to prison officer education in providing courses on psychology and sociology in collaboration with Millbank College of Commerce.

The unemployed, women's studies and community arts also represent areas of programme innovation. Sixty unemployed students were taken free of charge to the Liverpool Playhouse to see 'Educating Rita', by Willy Russell. In all, over 500 students from inner city discussion groups and courses went to see the play over tree nights - for many of them this was their first visit to a theatre.

This was one of the components in a series for the unemployed which covered Economics, Politics, Welfare Rights, Local History, Drama, Music, Architecture and Literature. Development from this is leading to a tutor organiser appointment to deal specifically with provision for the unemployed.

Collaboration with Community Arts exponents and Regional Arts Associations is leading to exciting new developments in provision which breaks down traditional barriers between educators and performers. This involves creative participation by students rather than simply passive assimilation.

Womens Studies has become an increasingly significant component in the W.E.A. Courses cover topics such as Women's History, Women and Manual Trades,

Positive Action for Women, the Changing Role of Women in Society, the Sociology of Childbirth. The Womens Education Advisory Committee produce their own national Newsletter and hold conferences as well as providing a forum for women's views.

One of the lessons are still have to learn along with all other adult educators is the art of communication with those whose interest has not been stimulated by our advertising techniques. With the tendency to specialize there seems to be a trend to enshrine knowledge in jargon, making it ever more inaccessible to the general public. Ritchie-Calder's lifetime career as a communicator is a model for us to look at. His lectures, with their lucid style and natural explanation of the meanings of technical or abstruse words when introduced are object lessons in a teaching style which avoids the dangers of being patronizing. There can be no complacency while the majority who suffered educational deprivation or received only basic education are still shut off from access to education opportunity. The WEA and the Open University are only just beginning to get together seriously in partnership at national level and it is to be hoped that we can in the next decade demonstrate the benefits of pooling resources and experience in fresh and new ways.

Can we rise to the challenge, and work towards the creation of that society which benefits all and leads to the full development of individual talents? The exciting possibility of revealing untold potential which school so often failed to reveal, of enabling artistic and creative faculties to flourish instead of having to immerse the whole of energies on industrial and bread and butter issues, is something we are geared to respond to. It is to be hoped that the majority have the perception to keep pace with the opportunities offered to them and that the democratic process can ensure a future for our children which puts continuing education in its rightful place, so that educational opportunities may be available to individuals as they mature and become aware of educational needs. The answers must lie in political and economic as well as educational decisions.

10

Case Studies in Non-formal Education for Rural Development

Introduction

The following 12 case studies were selected from 23 visited during a field study in Western Uganda from January to March, 1976. They represent a cross section of attempts at rural development being carried out by the personnel of the Roman Catholic Church in the four dioceses of Eastern Uganda.

1. Kabwangu School-Leavers' Resettlement Project

The project is situated in Bukuumi one of the oldest Roman Catholic parishes in Uganda. The people have had a long exposure to the influences of Christianity and to formal education, there are two large secondary and two large primary schools in the area. The students and staff of the former come from all corners of Uganda, and until recently there had been an important staff of expatriate teachers from Europe and America. The Parish borders on the district of Buganda, the richest part of Uganda, and it is close to the hub-town of Mubende, an important administrative, commercial and military centre. There has been a massive drift of the young to the local towns and the city of Kampala, and this drift, according to the local clergy is more acute in Bukuumi than in any of the other neighbouring parishes.

The project initially aimed at resettling those primary school graduates who were unable to continue their formal education, but it was eventually hoped to extend it to entire families, and to this end, the project organizers applied for an received 7,000 acres of land from the Uganda Government. In 1972, using subsidies offered by the Young Farmers of Uganda and the National Uganda Youth Organisation they were able to have the land surveyed and mapped at a nominal cost.

The project was to be organised in two phases, the first would use 1,000 acres of land and would train the young men in all aspects of their lives as farmers, in production, marketing, savings and credit, and it was hoped that by training an working together they would acquire attitudes of mutual trust so attempting to reduce mistrust, jealousy and lack if co-operation in the settlement proper. They were to be attached to this pilot project for two years before receiving land for resettlement. The second phase would consist of settling up to 400 families on the remaining 6.000 acres. Owing to the nature of the terrain, this would involve a massive bush-clearing exercise and the installation of a water supply.

When visited, 22 acres has been cleared under phase one of the project, and it had been found necessary to hire labourers, which might have been avoided has a tractor been available to the group. 25 young men of about 18 years are in the scheme and are growing both the traditional cash crops, cotton and coffee, as well as food crops, plantains, beans, groundnuts, potatoes, cassava and the like. It should be noted, that since the start of Uganda's depression, and the collapse in the coon distribution and collecting through the primary societies, the food crops have become far more rewarding economically than the traditional cash crops. Since 1973, the small subsidies for basic equipment, such as hoes, that the Government used to give have not longer been available, and the price has been driven up on the black market, practically the only place where they are available, by something in the order of 500% in a period of two years.

At present the settlers work communally, sharing the profits, but difficulties have led to questioning this method as the Banyoro traditionally worked on the basis of a family unit. To avoid marketing difficulties, they have established their own primary society but siting it four miles from the project to help the local population. By establishing the primary society, they are able to assure an equitable distribution of the little cash available, in the hope of avoiding theft, embezzlement and other misuses of funds common to primary societies in Uganda. Moreover, the organisers can control the sellers' incomes and introduce them to banking and saving their wages. Three member of the group were able to pay in a short space of time, the bride-wealth demanded by local custom. Such incentives give them dignity and show that they are not the failures that they thought they wee on leaving school.

Those who stay on the site of the project, are houses in buildings typical of the area but plans are underway to build a dormitory for them. Due to the present economic depression cement and corrugated iron sheeting have increased several hundred per cent in cost, and are available only on the black market, and even then supplies are extremely scarce, the settlers are making their own bricks and titles, which they will use with a local red earth as mortar, reserving the cement for the pointing, thus weatherproofing the exterior of the building.

Cebemo has assisted the project since the beginning of phase on in 1974 by funding the transport and the building of the dormitory. Other funds from unspecified foreign funding agencies have been made available to facilitate the actual cultivation, but Cebemo have also shown themselves interested in phase two.

The project is organised by a member of the parish clergy of Bukuumi assisted by a full-time salaries employee. The settlers are helped by labourers, eight of whom are permanently employed by the project, although at busy times of the year, this number increases. For some time the labourers have preferred to be paid in kind rather than cash, which would formerly have been unheard of.

There are plans to give a wider training in various crafts and skills, carpentry, masonry, book-keeping etc. bur rather than set up a special training facility, use will be made of what already exists in the country.

Among the many difficulties noted by the organisers were lack of initiative, responsibility taking, planning and foresight. There was a fear of taking positions of leadership, of failure, criticism, suspicion as well as a mutual distrust which made co-operation difficult. Owing to the high productivity of the soil, the Banyoro do not need to cultivate extensive areas and consider anything more than two or three acres as a large 'farm'. They are reputed to be slow and procrastinating. Attempts are made to counteract this among the settlers by taking them in small groups to visit other areas in the country in the hope that this will stimulate them.

2. Leadership training and basic adult education in rural areas

Fr. Gerard Salome has worked for 40 years in Uganda, most of the time in rural areas. Throughout this period his appraisal of the people's needs led him to start various courses in adult education aimed at training those the considered as natural leaders, or those that the community considered as their own leaders. The courses given were intended as resource material that the leader could use, or as a means of forming leaders. His basic philosophy was that leaders are formed through their contact with and formation of others, and he tried to stimulate those who took the courses to reflect on the inadequacies of their own situation and to encourage them into trying to ameliorate it. Although basically intended for leaders, the courses were open to all who wanted to take part. They were sometimes given to select groups, such as teachers or civil servants, or to more general groups, either at the suggestion of the organiser, or in response to a request for them

A series of talks would be given on a variety of subjects, of which there were two main categories as mentioned above, background knowledge for leaders and the skills that Fr. Salome considered necessary and information on the betterment of their daily lives. Out of these talks, a question and answer period or a discussion would generally evolve. Insistence was made on taking notes, otherwise the course was considered to be a waste of time.

At the beginning, some forty years ago, the Organisation of these courses was very informal. Religious services were used to bring to the attention of the local population that there would be a series of talks which usually took place in a chapel, in a school, if there was one nearby or under the proverbial mango tree. At that time, Fr. Salome would simply answer any sort of question that was asked in an attempt to find out which subjects interested the people most of all, but over the years it has become more structured with fixed times and premises, with the groups selecting from the list of subjects available what they want to discuss. However, the course remains essentially mobile, and for this reason Fr. Salome has never insisted on the building of special centres to house the courses, using whatever was available.

The course was usually given by Fr. Salome himself, with the help of someone else who has done one previously, of he would be able to call on some of his colleagues. It should be noted however, that he received little encouragement of help from his fellow clergy who were more interested in schools and the education of children, rather than that of adults.

This was essentially a low cost activity, and no money was requested or ever received from foreign based funding agencies. What little funding was needed was usually raised locally, and in many cases contributions from those following the courses were adequate.

During his last posting, which lasted until the end of 1975, he was giving courses every two or three months on request. They lasted generally two days and were attended on average by 50 to 60 people Apart form attendance not-taking was quite extensive, and the groups appeared interested and asked a large number of questions, and it should also be noted that they paid for his transport to and form the parish centre to the site of the course.

Courses given many years previously were still remembered and he is attributed as being the inspiration behind the foundation of a large co-operative growers and marketing society, established in the mid-fifties and is still flourishing. Other attempts, have been less successful, nothing remains of the project despite active Government support.

3. Kakindo farm training project

Kakindo is a remote and isolated area, and as a result it has received less than its fair share of development with fewer than average schools or medical units.

The project had tow objectives, to try out certain innovations in breeding and raising small domestic animals such as rabbits, pigs and chickens; cattle, both dairy and 'draught, were added at a later date. Secondly, if the first objective was successful, to encourage the local population to raise such livestock. A training programme was set up to help those who showed interest.

From the outset the organisers wanted to make the project self-supporting by establishing the farm on a sound economic footing. This led them to concentrate on the production of eggs and chicks, they therefore imported from Kampala the Capital, some 170 miles away, all the poultry feeds, and they installed an incubator to hatch the eggs and sell chicks locally, demand for both was always extremely high and could never have been met without a large-scale commercial enterprise.

Pig raising was also extremely successful. Hitherto the local population were not noted pork eaters, although there were no taboos forbidding it. Due to the difficulties involved in keeping pigs and their corresponding absence, the local population was simply unaccustomed to pork. Feed was bought outside to supplement what could be provided locally. The pork was sold locally or to hotels 60 miles distant.

Large forest areas infested by tsetse fly, and the presence of the brown tick the carrier of East Coast Fever made cattle rearing even more difficult, which explains the total absence of cattle in the area. With proper care, however, the cattle that were introduced survived and there was a growing demand for milk

The raising or rabbits never went further than the project, no sales of rabbits were made locally.

The training programme was given on the job under the direction of an experienced farm manager who had been trained by the priests themselves. The trainees were also given classes in literacy and numeracy. It should be noted however that these were often very young children, both boys and girls who had come to the parish for religious education.

The control and management of the farm was in the hands of the clergy who organised and planned it in detail. They saw to the preparing and buying of material and to the marketing of the produce. The farm manager looked after the running the farm and arranged the daily chores of the students. The literacy and numeracy classes were provided by nuns who were themselves Africans. When the control of the farm was handed to the parish council, as had been the intention form the start, it started to fail:

the transfer may have been made too quickly and without sufficient preparation. The idea was evidently firmly fixed in their minds that this was the "fathers'" farm, as they were not involved directly either in its foundation or development. However it should be borne in mind that the transfer took place at the beginning of Uganda's depression with the growing scarcity of commodities and hyper inflation which made the project uneconomic. To all intents and purposes it was abandoned in 1975, although the present parish staff keeps up a minimum on an imperimental basis in the hope of starting when conditions in the country in general improve.

Existing buildings were used and adapted. Every attempt was made to use local materials in laying out the animals' quarters

Originally capital came from a variety of foreign sources, but when increasingly larger amounts were needed as the project progressed and developed Cebemo started funding it. As the depression depended more and more, funds earmarked for capital development were used to cover recurring costs. Local support was limited to providing parish buildings and land, which in fact represented a considerable saving.

From many points of view the project was highly innovative and responded to real needs of the local population. A considerable group of people started raising chickens from the farm, but these efforts were restricted to domestic consumption and never became commercial. The raising of pigs proved more difficult as this entailed a greater capital outlay on the part of the farmers but there were local farmers who purchased piglets from the farm and raised them successfully. Cattle proved the most difficult of all because of the high costs involved and apart from the project itself, no one started raising cattle. There was no interest at all in breeding rabbits although this would have been the least expensive of all.

As this livestock required a great deal of care, it would have been interesting to see what changes in attitudes would have been required, or were acquired on the part of the successful farmers. Secondly, it would have been interesting to see which level of village society adopted the innovations, the salaries or non-salaries, the levels of education, etc. in an attempt to discover which group the project was directly helping and whether or not the project was giving an opportunity to the wealthy to become even weather.

4. Kyakatara community

Situated amidst the private and para-statal tea estates of Tooro, Kyakatara community was founded by Fr. Peter Cornelisse, a Dutch Trappist monk searching to live a contemplative life in rural Africa. He arrived in Kyakatara in 1967 and began to contact the local people through visits and celebrating the Roman Catholic liturgical services. He was struck in particular by the social problems of the migrant workers ad the fact that nothing was being done for them.

The project was originally an attempt to establish a community life for families, young men an women, but it has changed its objective and at present is concentrating on training in various rural skills, although a basic form of community life is maintained. It is open to anyone, between the ages of 18 and 30 without distinction of sex or religion. The one condition imposed is the completion of primary school education.

Fr. Cornelisse acquired from the Government half an acre of land and started working with the help of hire labour to build a hut for himself and a small building which serve as a social centre, classroom and church. By 1971 when he left or leave in Holland, he had a small group and 120 acres of land to farm. On his return he discovered that although the farm was running well, the community had broken down. He decided to start again with those who were left, laying more stress on the community aspect; they has common kitchens, dining rooms, recreation facilities and dormitories. Although he is due to leave once more on leave he is afraid to do so for fear that the community might suffer another and irreparable breakdown.

Owing to the large size of the farm and the small number of participants labour has to be hired and the men of the community are obliged to restrict their activities to the supervision of this labour force. The young women are mainly dedicated to social work, schools or clubs for women. A regular timetable is adhered to throughout the day with classes in Swahili, home economies, handicrafts, animal husbandry, music, agriculture, bible study and religion; there are also discussion groups.

The land is suitable only for tea and pasture owing to the high soil acidity, experiments have been tried in growing fruit and vegetables but these proved unsuccessful, eventually they plan to turn the whole farm over to livestock. A swamp is being reclaimed and will be used as a fish farm.

The concepts involved in this project have fired the imaginations of funding agencies in Europe and North America which have given comparatively large sums of money for capital development of the project, but their interest is limited to skills transfer and little to attitude change. The farm has already begun to bring in an income, and his pays the salaries of the labourers, but contributes as yet little to the community's recurrent expenditure, which is met by Fr. Peter's home community in Holland as their contribution to help the world's poor.

Fr. Peter works alone and cannot find anyone willing to take over his post should he have to leave. He realises that most of the other members of the clergy consider him an unrealistic dreamer and he has accepted the fact that there is little interest in his project on the part of the local bishop.

The major difficulties that confront such a project stem from existing attitudes to life and work. Community living is a concept that is unknown among the Batooro who count the major values as being the possessing of homes, land, wives and children. Individual needs and interests absorb everything in the struggle for existence and survival. Communities exist only at the level of the family, and even here very often only between the mother and the children, the father appearing almost as a stranger among these close-knit group. Moreover there is a great deal of selfishness, jealousy, conservativeness, irresponsibility, fatalism, superstition, lack of foresight and planning; their feelings of love and hate are equally superficial and temporary. It is difficult to find subjects of discussion that interest them, when Fr. Peter tries to encourage them to raise such points he meets with apathy and intertia, and feels that there can be little initiative for change coming from within the conservative, rural community. Their cultural values remain a mystery to him.

At the time visited, the community consisted of 28 young men and women. Six young men had completed four years with the community and have left to work, and are doing well farming on their own small plots. Two more are preparing to leave the community. Those who have left often return to visit their friends and fell immediately at home, and while away maintain an interest and contact with the centre.

It is interesting to note that although this is basically educational in nature, it is always referred to as a socio-economic project. This is a way of thinking that is generally shared among those who organise such projects as well as the funding agencies in Europe, they apparently do not wish to have their projects identified with the educational world but with the economic and social, which would seem to indicate not just a limited view of education, but also subconsciously a dissatisfaction with the school system.

A second point that this project brings out is that in general agricultural training and livestock raising is reserved for boys, and home economics for the girls.

5. The training of unemployed girls in rural Africa

After being supported by their parents throughout their primary school girls who cannot continue their education into the secondary level are often sent to find employment as house girls or in the bars and lodging houses of the district capital, often falling into prostitution. Professional employment for young women is generally open only to those who have completed four years of secondary school education.

The project was started with some 40 girls. Using

parish facilities subjects like needlework, sewing, handwork, crafts, child care, first aid, hygiene, English, typing, and religion were taught. The programme offered was free and was organised like a school with the girls attending from eight in the morning until four-thirty in the afternoon, an following a set timetable. It evolved into a two year course with 40 girls entering each year. Using the parish hall caused certain difficulties as a continues stream of visitors caused interruptions and destructions.

A nun was detached to look after the project; she organised the classes and found help from among the various other schools an institutions in the neighbourhood. This has helped the project financially, but they still find great difficulty purchasing the necessary materials for the school even though they sell most of what they produce.

The project seems to be very popular, applications run at double the number that could be accommodated, with some of the girls walking seven miles each way to attend. As a result, Misereor has promised funding but together with the local bishop has imposed certain conditions upon the project. First it must move from its present location close to an important hub town, to a sit some 30 miles distant in a more rural area. The annual intake will be raised to 60 per annum, and a three year course will be offered, the girls will board rather than commute from home. Attached to the school will be a farm which it is hoped will make the school self-supporting. This should also make good a major deficiency as women play an important role in the country's agricultural life. There is no evidence however that such radically different proposals will make the project any more successful than it has been in the past.

It would appear evident that this project responded to a need as is witnessed by the numbers applying for entry. It's adoption by a wealthy funding agency which is imposing its own conditions could result in a certain loss of its adaptability to respond to needs, and it could end up like a school with many of the formal system's problems.

The new phase of the project will be situated in 1, 270 acres of land which seems extraordinarily large for only 180 girls. This could cause planning and management difficulties and would call for a large capital outlay. One wonders what kind of an image this might project for the Church.

6. Butiiti parish tomato growers

The precise origins of this project are untraceable. The organiser, a young American priest has previously tried to implement projects helping his parishioners, but without much success. Possibly as a result of working in the parish vegetable garden, he discovered himself helping small groups of boys and girls to grow tomatoes and was surprise both their industry and their success Using the existing parish structure he was able to interest other groups of young people, and adults to such an extent that in the space of about three years he had gardens in 19 different sections of the parish, and in some of those sections there was more than one garden. There are no precise statistics to show how many people are involve, but at the parish centre for example, there wee 110 individual growers, but it must be admitted that this was the largest group of all.

Although the method of working varies from place to place, essentially the following pattern held good everywhere Land was provided by the parish, and all those who wanted to grow tomatoes paid a fee of 5/- to joint the society. Each person was given a plot of land for which he was responsible, and no attempt was made at co-operative or communal cultivation, in fact based on past experience this was actively discouraged, although there was no objection to small groups of two or three persons sharing one plot. Under supervision of a leader the land was cultivated and seed beds prepared by the grower. Seeds were distributed, planted and the shoots transplanted. Spraying was assiduously carried out particularly after each rain which was a critical period and might explain why the growers had so little success in their own gardens. Weeding and cleaning of the plots was carried out by the growers individually and they also harvested the crop and used it our sold it on the local market.

The training was simple, practical, and was limited to on the job instruction. In order to do this certain days and times were set aside when everyone would come and complete a specific task under supervision, in this way the instructor did not have to waste time repeating the same thing over an over again. It also helped to keep a check on those who did not turn up as weed infestation spread very rapidly. Spraying with pesticides was facilitated by the fact that all the plots were grouped together, and the people could see the effect that it was having.

As the plots were on parish land, the clergy could make regular checks as they carried out their normal pastoral activities. Furthermore the regular monthly meetings held at the parish centres helped exchange ideal and information as well as help solve problems together. No other personnel were involved and no salaries had to be paid.

This was a low cost activity, money was required for seeds, insecticides, pumps, spares, and fertilizers. Although each farmer paid 5/-, this was a nominal fee, and no attempt was made to see if this covered costs for the year. Extra funds were raised on a private basis in the United States from which country, Fr. Potthast the organiser, originated. With two seasons per annum, the farmers were able to increase their incomes by up to 65%.

There were a number of problems, it was difficult to convince the farmers that the spraying was all important, and had to be done after each rain, even if they had sprayed only five minutes before it started raining. Many parents were unwilling to let their children join in until they themselves realised how economically advantageous the project was. Problems were also caused by lack of trust, stealing, lack of co-operation of leadership, this latter was particularly noticeable in villages which were remote from the parish centre. Difficulties were also created by the conservativeness of rural society, and their understandable unwillingness to take financial risks, Particularly spending time and money on preventative measures.

The number of gardens has grown and the adults are now more numerous than the children. There is evidence, unsubstantiated however, of a spread effect from the project to their own gardens, but no real survey has been made. In view of the success of the project, it is unfortunate that the chemicals needed for the spraying, as well as the fertilizers, pumps and spares, were no longer available at the time visited.

7. Kaiho group farm

The project started simply in 1968. Faced with the

increasing numbers of young men who had finished school. Wanted employment and could not find it, and yet were unwilling to work on their parents' farms. Most of those who came to join the farm were young men who has tried unsuccessfully in the towns but has returned to the rural areas.

The young men cleared two acres, but as it was in open savannah with large numbers of trees, they quickly become discouraged. In clearing the land, a Government tractor was hired which ploughed once but in spite of having been paid in advance for the second ploughing, did not return-this was not unusual. An attempt to turn over the soil by hand with hoes proved unsuccessful. Fr. Ampe, the organiser, decided to raise money for a tractor from sources outside the country, an this provided an important psychological boost. The farm now covers 150 acres of land, has four tractors and a large selection of modern implements. The 150 acres are cultivated with a mixture of food and cash crops.

The project has 20 members, 15 of whom form a nucleus. There are also 30 labourers, 10 of whom are undergoing supervision before being accepted into the main group. They work and live in common, with married members living in small houses on the project. A management committee is elected by the members, and there are strict rules drawn up by the group members themselves covering most aspects of their lives and their work.

All who work on the farm both participants and labourers are paid a daily wage which is the same for all irrespective of the job done. When the crops are harvested and marketed, the net profit is distributed among the participants of the project, who have in this way increased their earnings up to then times those of the surrounding farmers.

Most of the work is done mechanically. All training is given on the spot in response to immediate demands and needs. There are no classrooms, classes literacy or numeracy training, and no leisure facilities.

The financing for this project is relatively high and we found that exact figures could not be given. The project has become a bit of a showpiece, and it is apparently relatively easy to raise further funds from foreign based funding agencies, from which most of the financing has been derived. The farm, however, is now generating its own large income based on the growing, milling and marketing of maize. At present maize flour, as indeed any food crop, is much in demand in Uganda.

The land upon which the scheme is run is owned by the Church, and apart from anything else, in an area of growing pressure on the land, this is an attempt to put unused Church land to the service of the community. The group applied successfully for an additional there square miles of Government-owned land to extend the project. It is hoped to start several more farms rather than have one big one, using Kaiho as the model and the training ground for the new farms. Similarly, money generated by Kaiho will be used to fund the new farms and in this way create a revolving fund.

There are a number of problems, although the farm has proved itself economically as a financial success the group members, in the estimation of the organiser, still have a long way to go to appreciate the values of co-operation and group effort. In particular they still lack to a very great extent, the feeling that this is in fact their own farm, an they are the group owners, and not working for an employer - a number of the participants still dream of owning their own small plots. Another major difficulty is learning to handle and treat with respect, modern farm machinery. The tractor appears as such a huge piece of equipment and apparently so strong, that they do not see limitations to its use, which can have disastrous effects, particularly at a time when spares etc. have to come a long way from Kenya, it takes at leas a week's journey to purchase spares and other pieces of equipment.

In spite of these problems, and the lack of any sort of scientific survey, changes are noticeable in the participants' attitudes to co-operative work. The off-scheme farmers can and to compare their own results with those of the group farmers. There is however no rush to join the group, and some of those who do join grow discouraged by the project's remoteness and the hard work involved and leave.

8. Ibanda school-leavers

The aim of this project was to help primary school leavers in any way possible by giving them a chance to study for, and resist their secondary school entrance examinations, learn trades, or improve on their agricultural skills. It was started in 1972 with 30 primary school-leavers in he local parish hall. At present it accepts between 30 and 40 students a year, and has increase the range of subjects offered to include animal husbandry, carpentry, tailoring and recently a hammer mill has been installed which will provide the school with a source of income and training as hammer mills are becoming more and more common in the countryside.

Training is given both in the classroom and on the job. During the first year, the students are given an all round training and an introduction to everything that is attached to the scheme. The day is the organised into academic an practical training with classes given in English, maths, first aid, hygiene home economics, and civics. In the second year each student together with the staff decide the student's specialist subject and the whole of the second year is spent on this.

The staff consists of Sr. Sylvia Probst, a Roman Catholic Swiss nun who was the initiator an organiser of the project, together with an assistant director, there teaches for classroom work and three for the practical work, with clerks, field workers etc. A large amount of money has been raised from foreign funding agencies to erect and install the various buildings, as well as purchase the livestock. Building is done in permanent materials with little or no attempt at adaptation to local needs and circumstances, thus costs tend to be high. The produce sold from the project does not appear as yet to be able to cover the project's recurrent costs and money still has to come from outside. It is hoped that the hammer-mill and the production and sale of uniforms to the surrounding schools will help alleviate this.

Sr. Sylvia maintains that she needs to pursue details, encourage and cajole so that the project progresses as she desires. As with Kaiho, frequent long trips have to be made to Kenya to purchase the necessary requisites for the project, and as a result there are doubts to the project's viability if the organiser herself should leave, or should there be a breakdown in communication with Kenya. When Sr. Sylvia was on leave the project went through a very difficult period.

The lack of participation in the project of the surrounding villages gives cause for concern, and may be the reason for numerous thefts. As a result all livestock have to be night-paddocked thus increasing the expense.

Because of her work sister Sylvia has been able to build up excellent relations with national and district level government officials which has enabled her to obtain scarce supplies. Foreign funding agencies appear to be great admirers of her work as is witnessed by the amounts of money's that she is able to raise.

Of the 30 who started the course in 1973, 28 graduated in 1975 and all were able to find jobs or further their training. Two started off their own small business a tailors with loans form Sr. Sylvia to buy sewing machines and within the space of two months were able to repay the loans obtained. However the fact that Sr. Sylvia obtained a large amount of land with the intention of setting some of the graduates would seem to indicate that there are some doubts regarding their integration on their parents' land when they have completed the course. It would appear that the project in this particular instance appears to be prolonging a problem rather than solving it.

9. Self-help projects in Bubangizi Parish

In 1973 Fr. Bernard Lannoye realised that there was a lack of a rable land in the parish, more children were going to and staying longer in school, as a result there were fewer people producing food with more mouths to feed. More and better land was required. In the neighbouring district swamp reclamation had been practiced for a number of years, and Fr. Lannoye decided to try and encourage people to adopt the practice in his own area.

In January 1974 they started on the first swamp when 109 people joined in a campaign to increase production. Four labourers were hired to cut away the papyrus and dig the main drainage canals, these were men who had experience in swamp reclamation. After digging a main drain of two miles, 150 acres of land were available for cultivation.

The farming was done on an individual or family basis, but the produce was marketed co-operatively. The swamps being Government property, reclamation does not give automatic right of ownership. As a result those who have reclaimed the land must request ownership from the local officials. A problem was created here by religious prejudice as many minor chiefs were of a different religion from the majority of those active in reclaiming the swamp. It happened that many of those who applied for an received ownership of the reclaimed land were of the religion of the religion of the officials even though few of them had participated in the land reclamation.

In general the land is rich in humus, fertile and if drained properly remains humid without becoming waterlogged. A wide variety of crops are grown including sugar cane. This was not an innovation in the area, but it is hoped to produce jaggery and later rough, brown sugar Under Amin, Uganda has gone from a sugar exporting country, to one where sugar is practically unobtainable.

The work is arranged among the participants themselves under the direction of the elected leaders and committee members. Individual growers hire labour at specific times of the year, during the harvest for example.

To a very great extent the project is self-financing, but a certain amount of help is needed from the outside, particularly in view of the present depression in Uganda. Hoes and weeding forks are no longer freely available in the shops as they once were.

Although the people see the need for swamp clearing they have to be continually encouraged an exorted to work. One group for example produced 40 bags of millet but waited for Fr. Lannoye to arrange the marketing. Due to lack of foresight they rarely see the need to produce more than demanded by their own immediate needs. A drought gave the project its initial impetus and there was definite lack of enthusiasm to continue the project when this passed, and it was only the enthusiasm of Fr. Lannoye that kept the work going.

It could have been argued that the need once met, the project could be allowed to die out, and that it was unnecessary for Fr. Lannoye to go to the lengths he did to keep the project alive. It must be taken into consideration that any slackening of pace would cause such deterioration in the reclaimed land, that within a matter of months the whole area could easily revert back into swamp again. Secondly, if this did not happen, then others, probably wealthier people such as teachers, civil servants or others with salaries who could afford to hire labour, would take over the reclaimed land and profit form the hard work of those who had originally needed the land. For the African farmer, the project having fulfilled an immediate need, could be abandoned, which to a European mind would seem wasteful in the extreme, and these latter would tend to keep the project going at any cost.

It could have been argued that the need once met, the project could be allowed to die out, and that it was unnecessary for Fr. Lannoye to go to the lengths he did to keep the project alive. It must be taken into consideration that any slackening of pace would cause such deterioration in the reclaimed land, that within a matter of months the whole area could easily revert back into swamp again. Secondly, if this did not happen, then others, probably wealthier people such as teachers, civil servants or others with salaries who could afford to hire labour, would take over the reclaimed land and profit form the hard work of those who had originally needed the land. For the African farmer, the project having fulfilled an immediate need, could be abandoned, which to a European mind would seem wasteful in the extreme, and these latter would tend to keep the project going at any cost.

10. The agricultural Centre, Nyarushkanje

The centre aimed at creating progressive farmers and accepted 18 year old students who had completed primary school education. A resettlement scheme was started to complement the centre, which also included a costing farm and coffee extension scheme.

The centre was organised like a school with regular classes, a timetable, and the students spends part of the day in class and part in practical training. The course was originally intended to last for two years, but was augmented to three, and then decreased once more to two years.

During this time they were given courses in economies, soil science, plant husbandry, animal husbandry, English, maths, general science, geography, civics and history. At a later date the following were introduced: English language, chemistry, physics, biology: co-operatives, and religion, reflecting a swing to a more academic approach. The standard expected on completion was that of the City and Guide (London) in tropical agriculture. The centre was run by two German lay Volunteers and two Ugandan nationals.

The students Worked on the costing farm where experimental work was carried out in the form of sensibility studies, it also served as a model farm. The extension service in which the students participated was carried to local farmers to help them produce more and better coffee. And instruction was given in weeding, spraying, pruning, as well as encouraging the farmers to grow alternative varieties.

The resettlement scheme was started to help the graduates who were unable to put into practice what they had learned on their parents' farms If the time spent at the school was not to be wasted, It became obvious that they spent at the school was not to be wasted, it became obvious that they would have to be given their own plots of land, as well as loans in the form of tools, seeds, fertilizers etc. A basic capital outlay was calculated which had to be repaid in five years after a three year grace period had clapsed. A special society was set up to market the corps and to assure the repayment of the loans, and it was set up to market the crops and to assure the repayment of the loans, and it was hoped to attract 80 to 100 farmers with arabica coffee as their main corp. Each participant had to bring two participant had to bring two porters to help him, and a German agriculturalists supervised the whole scheme. In the event only 10 agreements were made before the scheme was closed down, and none of the ten had received the full amount planned.

The project was funded jointly by the Dices of

Mbarara and Misereor. The latter paid one third of the capital costs as a grant, one third as a loan, and the diocese had to find the remaining third. Practically speaking, for the diocese had no locally generated funds for this type of work, all funding would come from outside the country. As against this however the diocese was able to put at the disposal of the centre 96 acres of land. Funding continued to be a problem, and the diocese was unable to continue the support of the project which was the main reason for its closure.

There were other reasons however, it had been founded on the expectation that the Uganda Government would be interested in it and would grant-aid it. Aid that time, however, in the late sixties, the Government was more interested in secondary school education, and had closed down other agricultural school education, and had closed down other agricultural schools. Yet another element was religious prejudice which was particularly bitter at this time, and in this particular area, and Ministry officials, particularly of education were not willing to help Catholic foundations. As a result of this, little help was given to Nyarushkanje. 11.

In general the students came because they could not find another way of furthering their education, and on graduation, instead of becoming progressive farmers, tried to obtain salaried employment in the agricultural sector. Farming, associated as it was with peasant, subsistence farming, was considered beneath the dignity of an educated person. Furthermore, as became apparent, they would never have been allowed to carry out the innovations that they were taught on their parents land.

The resettlement scheme was closed, not on any

merits or demerits of its own, because the centre was closed. No attempt was made to continue or extend the scheme without the centre.

11. Women's Rural Training Project: Rwanyina

This project was situated in an extremely backward area of the country, and it was to serve as a pilot project for the rest of the diocese. The aim was to help women in an area where they are not only more backward than their sisters in other parts of the country but where their social position was even more menial.

In a first phase the organiser of the project visited the parish bringing attention to general problems and the need for women's education. The second phase consisted of a team with three local leaders, two men and a woman, plus the organiser, the Rev. Fr. Tomaino. Their aim was to sensitise the population to the extremely low literacy rate; in one village for example only sixteen people could read out of a population of 1,600. They tried to found women's clubs among literate women in an effort to enlist them to teach literacy to other women. One of the major difficulties that had to be overcome was persuading the husbands to let their wives come to literacy classes. The Third phase would have the women coming to the parish centre to follow courses under the instruction of a nun and local community development officers. The fourth phase was to found a permanent centre where women would be trained be use sewing machines and at the same time be given courses in a whole range of subjects helpful to them in their everyday lives. Sewing machines were purchased and placed in two centers under the close supervision of the parish energy and a full-time teacher. After two weeks the girls were already familiar with the machines and by the third were producing simple garments.

40,000 posters showing the letters of the alphabet, dipthongs etc. were printed and sold, as were 45, 000 booklets at costs that covered the expenses. These were used in the traditional literacy campaign-type programme, and in one area 400 certificates were given where the Government literacy teachers had failed to make any impact whatsoever.

Funding for the project came from a variety of sources, all of them out-side the country. Costs could be kept to a minimum as much of phrases one and two coincided with the normal pastoral activities of the organisers of the project and local chapels and schools were used to give the courses. Money had to be sought for the sewing machines and to build the centres, which could also be used for a multitude of other functions.

When the organiser left the project, it came to a halt. Those who followed him either did not share the same interest or did not have the energy of the organiser who usually worked alone and independently from his colleagues. Furthermore, due to the deteriorating circumstances in the country, the sewing machines could not be repaired when they had to be. The present incumbent, in spite of these difficulties, is trying to revive the project.

It should be noted however, that tailoring the Uganda has traditionally been the work of men. It is only recently and then only in the factories of Kampala and Jinja that women have started this work. Needless to say, very few, and in this area probably no-one, is able to purchases a sewing machine for his or her own private use. Moreover, the costs of materials have escalated and cloth is not available in the quantities that it used to be due to manufacturing and import difficulties.

12. Makiro Parish Milling Co-operatives

The primary objective of this project was to encourage maize growing in an area where the plantain is the staple diet and in so doing provide an important dietary supplement. One of the major drawbacks lay in the hard work and time involved in grinding the grain into flour in a pestle.

Moreover, with machine milling, other grains such as millet, sorghum and hard root crops like cassava could also be ground. The organisers of the project also wanted to start milling on a co-operative basis so that profits could be shared out among as many users and producers as possible, rather than have it accrue to a small group as had hitherto been the case.

A pilot project was set up and a small secondhand mill was used to see if such a project would work. As this provide a success the clergy of the parish were given a loan to start a mill with a 30 hp engine. Three months after this installation the loan was repaid in full.

Encouraged by this initial success, the clergy of the parish started to encourage other centres to go into co-operative milling. Each farmer was asked to bring 100/- as his share and when enough money had been raised, a mill and engine were be purchased, and housing and stores built. Sometimes the co-operative society would collect enough to buy a small mill, and out of the profits buy a larger one. In other cases members succumbed to the temptation to distribute profits before any form of improvement could be made.

Each co-operative had its own board and employed its own miller-cum-book-keeper. The accounts are checked regularly by an official of the Ministry of Co-operatives. All funds are raised locally, but present circumstances, particularly the need to purchase new mills, engines and spares outside the country has led the millers to become even more dependent on the clergy to procure these for them with foreign exchange which only the clergy, with European connections, can obtain.

There are now 13 co-operative societies, and with 25 mills in operations, some of the societies have more than one mill. This co-operative effort has progressed to such an extent that there is no longer room for private enterprise, and the few who did start out alone have had to sell to the co-operatives as farmers preferred to do business with the group mills. At the beginning it was difficult trying to convince people to trust one another sufficiently to contribute money, but the idea of co-operatives effort appears to have taken hold, for not only were the later co-operatives easier to start, but the co-operative ideal is being espoused in other fields. In one case the parish has been able to set up a co-operative based on saw-milling and the production of furniture, in the process founding a rural-based cottage industry. On the other hand, a few of the co-operatives are such in name only, and in reality are companies. The former are groups of farmers who own the mill and who mill their own produce as well as that of others, the latter are mills owned by groups of non-farmers, teachers, civil servants and other paid employees, who put their money together to buy a mill and pay someone to run it for them, without using it themselves. In the case of Makiro both exist, but the former appear to be more successful and are run and managed better than the latter. Whereas the Government is again the multiplicity of small units, and closed down all the small cotton Jinneries and coffee hulleries,, combining them into larger units, these small mills supposedly less economic and efficient have proved to function better than the larger ones which are more impersonal. In the large units there is more embezzlement, cheating and falsified book-keeping. In the smaller units, where each one knows the other, more unconscious social control is practiced.

This does not mean to say that these smaller units do not suffer from the same difficulties as the larger ones, on the contrary, there is always an element of mutual distrust, jealousy and theft. Mills have been sabotaged, and profits have been distributed too quickly. In eases of theft when the culprit has been discovered, they are rarely dismissed and little apparent action is taken against them-it may be that village society has other ways of dealing with the problem.

As with kaiho, the lack of experience in dealing with large mechanized units, and their complexity gives rise to a number of problems. Machines are mishandled and maintained badly, and the difficulties of obtaining foreign exchange to purchase spare parts in Kenya also creates a major problem at present. The few spares available in Uganda are sold at vastly inflated prices, and the quality is extremely poor.

Uganda's co-operative laws are excellent and would be of great help if they were put into practices. Unfortunately corruption, laziness, incompetence, inefficiency and the lack of transport enabling the officers to travel from place to place, constitute maior drawbacks to the system.

It was the opinion of the co-operatives' chief initiator that traditional and rural society is too static and conservative and that there could be little hope of change coming from within it. Progress could only come from contact with the outside, as is shown here.

1. Reference will be made on a number of occasions to this. Since the explosion of the Asian community in 1972, Uganda's economic and commercial life has deteriorated to an alarming extent with hyperinflation, scarcity of commodities, hoarding, profiteering, smuggling, etc. We do not believe that this is due to incapacity of the African businessman, who in our experience is an good as the Asian or any other, but mainly to the fact that the Government of President Amin will not given them the chance to carry out normal business nativity. Most of the businesses were grabbed by incapable people whose only qualification was their army rank.

2. Cebemo is a Dutch funding agency to which both the Dutch churches and Government contribute.

3. Due to the scarcity of the most basic commodities, salt, sugar, soap, matches, etc. and their cost on the black market, payment for work in cash has become meaningless. Many workers prefer to be paid in these goods, and system has been worked out, upon which both worker and employer agree.

4. Some of the subjects included in this list: public speaking; the founding, running and organising of clubs and groups: preparing, polling and voting in elections; debating; political action; discussion of racial, social and political conflicts; child and adult education: the role of the individual and the

community in social life: resolving conflicts in the social order; the place and role of work in society; just remuneration and the rights and duties of workers; the State; the Family; The Church; Trade Unionism; class conflict in society; trade; private and common good; the use and abuse of alcohol; distribution of wealth; rights and duties of ownership, capitalism and its problems. Most of these subjects were taught from the specific point of view of the ethical and social teaching of the catholic church.

5. This included: flooring in houses, improved kitchen stoves a potter's wheel made from a bicycle, building blocks, planting and care of the eucalyptus as a source of firewood and building material, cleanliness and hygiene in the home, book-keeping and simple accounting, improved farm tools, animal husbandry.

6. According a report by the F. A.O. 'African Agricultural Development', New York, 1966, pig breeding in the tropics is more expensive and more difficult than poultry breeding.

7. 'Para-statal' meant that the factory and estate were owned partly privately by the Ugandan Government with the latter owning the controlling share. This of course changed in December 1972 when amin confiscated and nationalised the factories.

8. Misereor is the Development Agency set up by the German Catholic bishops to help the world's poor, the West German Government also contributes to it.

9. In Migrants and proletarians: Urban Labour in the Economic Development of Uganda', welter Elkan talks of circular migration the rural Uraban drift, and

the drift back to the rural areas of those who could not find employment. Most of the priests and other Church workers interviewed had witnessed this, only the Fathers in Bukuumi stated that they had no evidence of it, and that the drift was one way only.

10. Since this section on Ibanda was written we have learned that Sr. Sylvia has had to leave Uganda on the grounds of her own personal security.

11

The Dynamics of Continuing Professional Education

There can be Little argument that the professions are central to the functioning of American society. They teach our children, manage and account for our money, settle out disputes, diagnose our mental and physical ills, guide our businesses, help many of us mediate our relationship to God, and fight our wars. Their members represent over a quarter of the work force and are the primary decision makers for society's major institutions. The work of professionals is important, not only because of their technical skill, but also because they define to a great extent the problems on which they work. As a result they have the power to define our needs. For example, educators decide what our children will learn as well as how. Physicians decide who is healthy and who is healthy and who is not. The special place of the professions in society results as much as their symbolic leadership as from the application of their technical knowledge and skills.

From, the beginning of the move to organize

professional groups, both their leaders and the public have assumed that practitioners would continue to learn throughout their working lives. They were right in this assumption: Professionals learn through books, discussions with colleagues, formal and information educational programs, and the rigors of everyday practice. One of these forms of learning, formal continuing education programs, has increased dramatically in the past quarter century. Although no precise data are available, knowledgeable observers estimate that billions of dollars are spent annually to provide and attend such programs. As a result, organized and comprehensive continuing education programs are evident today in engineering, accounting, law, medicine, pharmacy, veterinary medicine, social work, librarianship, architecture, nursing, management, public school education, and many other professions.

A great deal of evidence indicates that most professions now embrace the importance of lifelong professional education. For example, medicine, perhaps more than most professions, has recognized this for many years. This president of the Association of American Law Schools recently chided those who seek a solution to the problem of lawyer proficiency by focusing solely on law schools, saying that "legal education is a lifelong process that requires a joint effort by the law schools, the bench and the bar, and individual lawyers". A prominent member of the library profession said that even fifteen years ago the discussion of the term *continuing education* was thought unimportant by leaders of the field. Yet, in 1985, at the first World Conference on Continuing Education, "continuing library education was advocated as an essential element of a librarian's lifetime education".

These visions reflect the increasing amount of attention being paid to continuing education in the professions. Many professions have a system of accreditation for providers of continuing education. All fifty states use participation in continuing education as a basis for relicensing members of certain professions. Phillips lists sixteen professions that are regulated in this way. The future of continuing education appears to be headed toward rapid growth and development. Many people believe that systems of continuing education will be built that rival the professional preparation programs now in existence. The leaders of most professions would probably agree that "what we hardly dare prophesy today will be seen by later generations as efforts to achieve a manifest necessity". This increasing attention in seen by many as a positive development of continuing education.

This focus has also magnified the widespread shortcomings in the practice of continuing professional education. Houle does not overstate the problems of continuing education today when the describes this typical program: "Faculty members who can be persuaded to do so give lectures on subjects of their own choosing to audiences they do not know, who have assembled only because they want to put in enough hours of classroom attendance so that they can meet a relicensure requirement". Furthermore, these simple activities are expected to improve the performance of professionals whose practices are full of complexities, uncertainty, and conflicting value judgments. Given these conditions, the great concern in the professions with the quality of continuing education should not be surprising.

Continuing education for the professions

Due to the increasing attention given to continuing

education in the professions, a new field of educational practice has come into existence. This field is becoming increasingly differentiated from the educational practices of preprofessional education. For example, many people think of themselves and are considered by others to be continuing medical educators or continuing engineering educators, when, in fact, they may not have had any experience in the preprofessional education of the groups with whom they work. The evidence for this movement is unmistakable. For example, several journals in North America are devoted exclusively to the theory and research of continuing education for specific professions. There is the *Journal of Continuing Education in the Health Professions, the Journal of Continuing Social Work Education, the Journal of Continuing Education in Nursing,* and the *Journal or Nursing Staff Development.* In addition, there is a trend for continuing educators in specific occupation to form interest groups within their national professional organizations, such as the American Nurses Association. Other educators choose to form their own associations, such as the Society of Medical School Directors of Continuing Medical Education, the Society for the Advancement of Continuing Education in Ministry, and the National Association of State Judicial Educators.

Within the professions the traditional view has been that the continuing education function must be directed by its own members, while the emerging view is that individuals trained in the field of continuing education have the most appropriate background for this function. While there is an increasing movement toward the emerging view, its adherents are still in a significant minority. One estimate is that of all the people who perform continuing education functions within the professions, 95 percent have been trained only in the content of their own profession. The remaining 5 percent either have their formal training only in education or have been trained both in their profession and in education.

Continuing education for the professions as a field of educational practice is quite young. As such, it is guided by concepts that have not been fully thought through or adequately tested. In fact, many of these concepts are holdovers from the models of preprofessional education, which should not be surprising given the academic background of most educators. However, with the entry of more individuals trained in the field of adult education, increasing attentiveness is being given to models and concepts of educational practice from that field.

The purpose of this books is to identify the elements of effective practice in continuing professional education. By making these concepts explicit, the author intends to stimulate an ongoing analysis and critique of practice. The most effective way to improve practice is for educators to understand the assumptions and principles that guide their work, examine whether they are the most useful ones, and change them when necessary. A small but growing literature base in continuing professional education itself serves as a useful point of departure for analysis. This literature has begun to synthesize the voluminous material that describes the research and practice base of continuing education for the individual professions. The literature in the individual professions additionally constitutes a rich resource for the study and practice of continuing professional education. This material is used selectively to illustrate the major issues that are common in the practice of continuing education across the professions.

As first step toward analyzing practice, it is necessary to make explicit the approaches being used to understand both the professions and continuing education. There is no commonly accepted way to approach these concepts; thus it is imperative that the assumptions underlying this book be stated that for the reader to evaluate.

What are the professions

In order to talk intelligently about continuing education for the professions as a field of practice, the differences between professions and other occupations must be examined. Without making this distinction, educators would be practicing in continuing occupational education or continuing education because their clientele would be undifferentiated from adult learners in general.

The problem of defining professions has a long and controversial history. The earliest effort to define a profession is generally considered to be by Flexner in 1915, and the most recent comprehensive analysis was by Friedson. As anyone who has examined the literature on the professions will readily attest, there is no commonly agreed upon answer to the question of what constitutes a profession. Rather, schools of thought with different approaches yield different answers. Because sociologists are no closer to an accepted definition now than in 1915, many have suggested that it makes no sense to try define the professions at all. Avoiding a conscious attempt at definition would promote the belief that professions are simply those occupations which have gained professional status. This determination is unacceptable to those who wish to think clearly and systematically about continuing education for the professions. The central tasks are to identify the major approaches to a definition, select one, and provide a rationale for the choice. Three approaches that have been identified in the literature are static, process, and socio-economic.

Static Approach. The oldest definitional approach was pioneered by Flexner, who believed "there are certain objective standards that can be formulated" that distinguish professions from other occupations. He identified the following six characteristics as essential for an occupation to claim professional status. Professions must (1) involve intellectual operations, (2) derive their material from science, (3) involve definite and practical ends, (4) possess an educationally communicable technique, (5) tend to self-organization, and (6) be altruistic. Others over the years have compiled the lists of attributes of a profession. Today many occupations are still applying these generic criteria to decide whether their occupation is a profession. This is particularly true for occupations that are striving for higher status, such as social work, school teaching, nursing, and early childhood education. This is called the *static approach* because objective criteria firmly discriminate between those occupations which are inherently a profession and those which are not. Once this distinction is made, it is unlikely that those which are not could ever develop into professions.

Since the 1960s the static approach has received such criticism that almost no one uses it who seriously studies professions as a concept. The major problem with this approach is the persistent lack of consensus about the criteria that should be used to define professions. For example, Millerson found twenty-three elements that were included in various definitions. Of the twenty-one authors used in his analysis, no single criterion was common to all of them. Furthermore, no two authors agreed that the same combination of criteria should be used to define a profession.

Johnson provides a systematic treatment of the reasons for this lack of consensus. In his view the fundamental problem arises at the starting point of this approach, which is that there are "true" professions that exhibit all of the criteria to some degree. The procedure of listing criteria without any explicit theoretical framework means that it is possible to apply particular criteria arbitrarily. The implication for continuing education is that, without any way to agree on the criteria that mark a profession, educators cannot have a clear idea of which occupations are professions and which are not.

Process Approach. Because of the problems inherent in the static approach, a different way of thinking about professions developed in the early 1960s. Hughes put in this way: "In my own studies I passed from the false question 'Is this occupation a profession?' to the more fundamental one, 'What are the circumstances in which people in an occupation attempt to turn it into a profession?". This *process approach* came into full flower then Vollmer and Mills used it as the organizing principle for their book on professionalization. This approach differs from the all-or-nothing-at-all style favored in the static approach by viewing all occupations as existing on a continuum of professionalization. Thus, the relevant question became Hoe professionalized is an occupation? It has been argued that all occupations go through a natural sequence in their passage to professional status although there is no consensus on this point. Another possibility raised by the process approach is that occupations can deprofessionalized, suggesting that the continuum is not a one-way street. A number of authors have explored this possibility for even the most professionalized occupations such as medicine and law. Kleinman argues that liberal protestant clergy have deprofessionalized their own role as a response to modernization, secularization, and religious pluralism. They have rejected the idea that ordained clergy are experts in religious matters and have replace it with a role that accepts egalitarian relationships with lay people. Although the process approach assumes that it is possible for a profession to deprofessionalize, it is generally not viewed as desirable.

An important assumption of the process approach is that no clear-cut boundary separates professions from other occupations. Vollmer and Mills state that professionalization is a process "that may affect any occupation to a greater or lesser degree". This is important for continuing professional educators because "all occupations seeking the ideals of professionalization are worthy of sympathetic study...". This approach avoids many of the pitfalls of the static approach because it recognizes the dynamic conditions of contemporary occupations structures. Also, by claiming that professions never reach a point of becoming an ideal profession, the rationale is established for both constant improvement and continuing learning.

Another positive aspects of the process approach is its emphasis on understanding the professions in relation to society. The process approach is based on the premise that the professions are necessary to the smooth and orderly functioning of society. In turn, society provides professionals with relativity high levels of money and status as a way of rewarding their highly valued with. However, by stressing the socially functional value of professional activity, this approach does not recognize the social inequalities that are a result of these rewards. These inequalities are usually interpreted as natural and even necessary to support professional work.

Because it does not deal critically with the social and economic consequences of professionalization, the process approach has been criticized as "a distortion of reality because it neglects a historical explanation which indicates that any given reward structure is the result of arrogation by groups with the power to secure their claims....". That is, the process approach does not seek to understand the professions in terms of their power in society. By failing to account for the processes by which professions gain and use their power and authority, it does not explain how occupations can come to be viewed as more professionalized.

Friedson concludes that the difficulties encountered in using the static and process approaches to define a profession stem from the same fundamental problem. Both attempt to treat a profession "as if it were generic concept with particularistic roots in those industrial nations that are strongly influenced by Anglo-American institutions"

Socio-Economic Approach. Several theorists argue that occupations in England and the United States have sought to be classified as professions since the late nineteenth century, whereas in western Europe, and even more so in eastern Europe, this activity has been nearly nonexistent. Friedson notes that the newer occupations of Europe "did not seek classification as professions to gain status and justify a market shelter; such an umbrella title inputting special institutional characteristics to them was not employed to distinguish them". Rather, the status and security of these occupations were gained by other means, such as protections provided by their governments.

Instead of striving to find a scientific concept that would apply to a wide variety of settings, several analysts have concluded that any profession is a "folk concept" that is historically and nationally specific. This approach contrasts dramatically with both static and process approaches and that no set of criteria is necessarily associated with it. There are only those occupations which are commonly regarded by the general public as professions and those which are not. As Becker argues: "Such a definition takes as central the fact that 'profession' is an honorific title...a collective symbol and one that is highly valued." Thus, a profession is determined by which occupations in a specific society of at a given historical time have achieved professional status and privileges.

Although this approach assumes that reality and meaning are socially constructed, it emphasis that "social construction is not a random process but a political war". Relatively high degrees of social and economic rewards are accorded they winners of this war. Professionalization is the process by which producers of special services constitute and control the market for their services. In this process, occupations attempt to negotiate the boundaries of a market for their services and establish their control over it. For this professional market to exist a distinctive commodity must be produced. Unlike industrial labor, most professions produce intangible goods in that their product is inextricably bound to the person who produces it. Therefore, the producers themselves have to be "produced" if their products are to be given a distinctive form. In other words, professionals must be adequately trained and socialized to provide recognizably distinct services. This process has been institutionalized in the modern university, which gives professions the means to control their knowledge base as well as to award credentials certifying that practitioners possess this recognizably distinct type of knowledge. Therefore, an occupation's level of professionalization can be assessed by the extent to which and political authorities accept its credentials an necessary to provide a specific type of service.

Professions in the United States. One approach to determining which occupations are accepted as professions by the public in the United States has been to use the categories developed by the federal Bureau of the Census. Although there is some disagreement about how to use census categories, the debate has been framed in such a way as to produce a least-restricted and a most-restricted approach to defining professional occupations. By presenting both of these approaches, the range of occupations that might be considered as clientele for continuing education for the professions can be delimited.

Much of the literature on census definitions has used the categories as they were defined in the 1970 census. Attention was focused on two major categories: (1) professional, technical, and kindred workers and (2) managers and administers, except farm workers. Some definitions in the literature use all of the occupations in both categories to represent the professions. Some use "new class" theory to identify the existence of a "professional-managerial class", while others attempt to formalize the perceptions of the general public. These definitions are the least restricted ones commonly used to identify professions in the census data.

Some assumptions must be made when extrapolating these definitions to the most recent census figures, because these two categories were rearranged for the 1980 census. In that census a new category was created: managerial and professional speciality. This classification combined the two previous categories, except that technical occupations were moved to another major category. Because the technical occupations have been used in much of the literature, they are included here.

Applying the least-restricted definition to the 1986 census figures produced an estimated of nearly 30 million professionals in the United States. Some of the more populous occupations, totaling over 1 million practitioners, are accountants and auditors, engineers, registered nurses, teachers, and health technologists and technicians. This collection of occupations made up 27 percent of the employed work force in 1986. In comparison to the total work force, of which 44.4 percent were women, women made up 43.8 percent of the professions.

Friedson criticizes this broad definition of the professions because of the great heterogeneity in these census categories in terms of educational background, income, and prestige. In its place he offers a more restrictive definition of the professions. For many of these occupations, particularly in the "executive, administrative, and managerial" category, very few had training or educational requirements that were mandatory. He argues that to be able to identify a reasonably homogeneous group of occupations as professional, a more restrictive criterion is necessary. Friedson proposes that for an occupation to be classified as a profession, some amount of higher education must be a prerequisite to employment. The rationale is that "formal knowledge creates qualification for particular jobs, from which others who lack such qualification are routinely excluded. Such a circumstances is likely to mean that those occupations have developed a coherent organization....that succeeds in carving out a labor-market shelter.....".

Using this criterion, most of the occupations in the "professional specialty" category are included, except for "writers, artists, entertainers, and athletes." Some of the occupations command high prestige and income, such as law and medicine, while others score relatively low in these areas, such as school teaching. Nevertheless, whether high or low in prestige, they have almost a complete labor-market monopoly for their services. In the "executive, managerial, and administrative: category, only three occupations are actually professions, according to Friedson: school administrators, including principles and superintendents; health administrators; and accountants. In the technical category, only health, engineering, and science technicians are included; airline pilots, computer programmers, and legal assistants are excluded. These occupations are not considered a profession, according to Friedson, because working in them does not depend on possessing higher education credentials. Applying this more restrictive criterion produces an estimate of 16.2 million professionals in the United States, almost 14 million fewer than produced by the least-restrictive definition.

Without a doubt, professions are an important social reality in American society. While there is no agreement on which occupations constitute that reality, we know its parameters. Somewhere between 16 and 30 million people in this country given the label of professional by the general public. This book is devoted to the practice of continuing education for this group of occupations.

A comparative approach to continuing education

In the rapid growth of continuing education, most educators have relied for guidance and models on the distinctive knowledge base and structures of a particular professional group. For example, most physicians, accountants, and lawyers would claim that continuing education should keep them up to data, a concept that is consistent with their preservice training in which they were given large amounts of information to remember for application in their practice setting. By relying on preprofessional training, each profession naturally concludes that its continuing education programs are unique to its own profession.

However, many people have noted the similarities of the continuing education efforts of individual professions in terms of goals, processes, and issues. Thus, the concept of "continuing professional education" begin to be used in the late 1960s to describe an identifiable field of study and practice. The early advocates for this *comparative approach* were adult and continuing educators who were struck by the similarities in the educational processes used by the different professions with which they worked. Houle's comparative study of seventeen professions convinced him that "certain dominant conceptions guide all of them as they turn to the task of educating their members and that they tend to use essentially the same kinds of facilities, techniques, and thought processes". The most important rationale for this movement is that the study of similarities across the professions can yield a fresh exchange of ideas, practices, and solutions to common problems.

The comparative approach to continuing education for the profession has a base in the literature as well as in the social organization of educators. Several books, numerous articles, and many conference reports have been published on the topic of continuing professional education. The way in which professional organizations organize themselves reflects an increasing awareness of continuing professional education. For example, two major associations of adult educators have specialized divisions devoted to continuing professional education. Finally, many graduate programs in adult and continuing education have a course or sequence of courses devoted to the special knowledge, skills, and issues necessary for effective practice in continuing professional education.

12

Being Effective in Continuing Professional Education

Throughout this book an attempt has been made to identify the elements of effective practice in continuing professional education. These elements include the ethical dimensions of practice, concepts of professionals both as learners and participants, the institutional context of practice, and approaches to program development and evaluation. Although these elements may be separated for analytical purposes, they do not exist in isolation in the real world of practice. Continuing educators see professionals as learners and as participants as they develop and evaluate programs, which they do within an institutional context and a particular ethical framework. Because these elements operate simultaneously in most practice situations, they must be synthesized into a coherent whole to understand and to improve practice.

In this final chapter these various elements are synthesized into a unified picture of effective practice in continuing professional education. The purpose is to offer a comprehensive statement of what constitutes effective practice, thereby providing the criteria to evaluate and improve current efforts in continuing professional education. These criteria may be used to evaluate individual or collective activities of many continuing educators working with any of the professional groups identified.

Continuing educators as professionals

The identification and analysis of the elements of effective practice flow from the assumption that continuing educators are engaged in a form of professional practice. Seven when program development was described as a form of professional work. This premise is now made explicit in order to explore its implications. The foundations of this exploration are the discussions of professional practice and knowledge in Chapters Two and Three. Thus, an understanding of effective practice for continuing professional educators should be consistent with the view of effectiveness in all forms of professional practice.

The functionalist, conflict, and critical viewpoint provide three fundamentally different understandings of professional practice. It was argued that the critical viewpoint offers the most accurate understanding of professional practice and should form the foundation of understanding continuing professional educators' practice. In choosing the critical viewpoint the functionalist and conflict viewpoints were rejected because they offer incomplete descriptions of practice.

Functionalist prescriptions for effective practice offer suggestions for good practice in such areas as assessing needs, developing objectives, assessing learning outcomes, and administrating institutional units. These prescriptions are generally in the form of guidelines or principles that are to be applied to situations faced by continuing educators. Take, for example, that shibboleth of good practice, assessing the needs of learners. The principle is often stated something like this: Sponsors of continuing education programs should utilize systematic processes to define and analyze the issues or problems of individuals, groups, and organizations for the purpose of determining learning needs. While this may seem like a worthwhile goal for practice, it offers little in the way of guidance to practitioners because it ignores the crucial element of institutional context.

To be sure, there is no shortage of statements of good practice that provide what must seem a rather obvious list of things continuing educators ought to be able to do. However, the existence of such lists assumes that there are standard contexts and problems to which these principles can be applied. Herein lies the fatal flaw, as discussed, continuing educators work in a variety of different situations that make radically different demands on their skills, knowledge, and judgment. One of the fundamental problems in conceiving of effective practice as the application of principles to situations is that each principle means different things and emerges as different practices in varying contexts. A major reason, then, that continuing educators reject textbook prescriptions for exemplary practice is that the principles are either vacuous or limited, or both.

To illustrate these points, take the example in which the continuing educator is planning a program for engineers on new techniques for designing nuclear power plants. The question to answer is: What would effective practice look like in terms of assessing the needs for this program? An important consideration in answering this question is the type of institution in which the continuing educator works. The context of a university continuing education unit provides a different set of constraints and opportunities for the educator than the power plant does for the training director. For example, the training director has direct access to the learners themselves, as well as records of their performance. Another consideration is the level of resources that the educator has available to conduct the needs assessment. Suppose the university continuing educator responds to a request from the training director for a program on the newest techniques in designing power plants. The educator knows that the training director did not conduct a systematic needs assessment and that no university resources are available to conduct one. Should his practice be judged as ineffective in this situation? What criteria would be used to do so?

Even this brief example should be sufficient to point out the shortcomings of the functionalist understanding of continuing education practice. Instead, as argued at the end of Chapter Two, continuing professional educators must operate within the critical viewpoint in order to provide a comprehensive understanding of continuing education practice and the means to improve it. The critical viewpoint asserts that practice cannot be understood as the application of standardized principles to well-formed problems because most situations faced by continuing educators are characterized by uniqueness, uncertainty, or value conflict. Like other professionals, continuing educators must make choices about the nature of the problem to be solved as well as how to solve it. Because continuing educators are continually making choices, as opposed to simply applying principles, the critical viewpoint stresses the need to be aware of the range of choices open to educators and the ways in which these can be made. The critical viewpoint provides a framework within which to describe effective practice in continuing professional education. It offers a rich account of practice and one that can help continuing educators to improve their work.

Understanding effective practice

Continuing educators' practice must be rooted in a coherent account of its ethical, contextual, and epistemological bases. All of these bases of practice are interconnected and are implicit in all forms of practice in which continuing educators engage. The next sections discuss each of the bases in more detail.

Ethical Basis of Practice: Because they seek to change individuals through their programs, continuing professional educators, like all educators, are engaged in a normative enterprise. Any attempt to change professionals is based on ideals of what they ought to be, to know, to do, or to feel. These ideals are rooted in continuing educators' beliefs about the goodness or rightness of the new course of action. Herein lies the ethical nature of practice, for educators continually make choices, often implicitly, about the ideals toward which their activities are directed. Therefore, practice can be judged as effective only with respect to a particular ethical framework, and it can be judged as ineffective if it is inconsistent with the tenants of the framework by which it is being evaluated.

Many continuing professional educators act as if there is consensus about the proper ends of professional practice. As a result, there is rarely any discussion of the ethical dimensions of their practice. Continuing educators are often blinded to the ethical implications of their work by the homogeneous value orientations of the environments in which they work. They are often unaware that they make ethical choices in their practice because everyone who may be involved in a particular situation agrees with those choices. Stripped of this ethical understanding, continuing educators are limited to using a paratechnical language to describe their practice, using words such as needs assessment, performance objective, collaboration, and teaching style. This provides at least a partial explanation for the current dominance of the functionalist understanding of professional practice.

In all professions there are differing, if not conflicting, ethical frameworks that guide the work of practioners. Examples were provided in Chapter Two. In the same way, continuing educators' practice is embedded in a variety of ethical frameworks. Every educative activity for which continuing educators have responsibility is a statement about the need for a particular form of technical knowledge, as well as a statement about the proper ends of professional practice. The ethical questions that are central to educational practice are: Why should professionals have this knowledge? To what ends will this knowledge be put? and What model of the learner should guide educational decisions? The most important decisions continuing educators must make in order to answer these questions are: Who should decide on the content of the activity? and On the basis of what criteria?

These ethical choices are not some abstract ideal, but are embedded in the very fabric of practice. Let us return to the continuing engineering education example in which the training director has asked the university continuing educator for a program on the newest techniques in designing nuclear power plants. By agreeing to deliver this program, the educator has made a series of ethical choices. For example, he believes that building power plants is a good thing and that the engineers need new knowledge to build them. He may not acknowledge having made these choices; instead, he might say he is basing his decision to offer the program on the need to generate income for the university continuing education unit. However, he cannot deny that the content of the program is consistent with a particular ideal about what society needs. His practice would be seen as effective if one agreed with this ideal and if the engineers attended the program and learned the new engineering techniques. However, his practice would be seen as ineffective if one did not agree with this ideal; for example, if participation in the program facilitates the goal of building nuclear power plants, and if one were opposed to nuclear power, then this practice would be seen as ineffective.

Our understanding of continuing education practice is impoverished by not discussing its ethical dimensions. Ethical understanding is central to the practice of all professionals and is an important criterion by which decisions are made in many situations. If continuing educators are to adequately understand and improve their practice, its ethical dimensions must be made explicit in the context of own practical knowledge, as well as in the ongoing of good practice in the continuing education literature.

Contextual Basis of practice: Continuing education practice is not conducted in a laboratory where all conditions are controlled except for the educator's actions. If this were true it would be reasonable to construct a description of ideal practices, the completion of which would produce specified results. As we know, however, practice is always conducted in a context composed of varying personalities, shifting expectations, conflicting goals, and limited resources. Because continuing educators' practice is rooted in particular sets of circumstances, it would be inappropriate to judge their efforts against some fixed ideal of good practice. Rather, to know whether practice is effective it must be judged by what is best in a given set of circumstances. Excellent practice cannot be characterized by a discrete set of knowledge of skills, but rather by an understanding of why educators do what they do when they do it. At the root of practice is not measurable techniques but judgment, which is itself a from of knowledge.

The primary context for continuing educators is provided by the institutional setting in which they practice. Continuing educators are not independent agents developing educative activities in ways they alone believe to be the most appropriate.Rather, their concepts of a target audience, how best to serve it, and what resources are available are conditioned by their particular institutional contexts. Their work is conducted within a discretionary framework set up by the goals and resources of the agency in which they work. As described in Chapter Five, there are four principal types of institutional contexts in which continuing professional education is provided. The continuing education unit in which practitioners work will have different functions depending on the type of institution in which it is located. Thus, its effectiveness will be judged in different ways. For example, many employing agencies use continuing education to improve professionals' performance, while others use it to generate income. Some functions may not seem ideal and may even contradict an educator's vision of what constitutes effective practice. Yet, within an institutional context, these different functions help to define the circumstances within which educators practice.

The contextual relativity of practice does not mean that all practice is equally good. It dies mean that practice can only be judged against what is best under the circumstances in which it occurs. Returning to the continuing engineering education example, let us ask whether the university-based continuing educator should have assessed the learning needs of the target audience. Let us assume that the training director asks for a program on the newest techniques of nuclear power plant design. To whether and what kind of needs assessment is required in this situation, more information is required. That alone illustrates the contextually relevant nature of the decision. It is easy to conceive of a set of circumstances in which the educator should have done a systematic needs assessment but did not. Perhaps a course is taught on techniques that cannot be implemented in the engineers; work setting. This continuing educator clearly can be judged as having engaged in ineffective.

It is possible to develop guidelines that can serve as orienting principles for effective practice. However, these guidelines must be *models of* practice in the sense that are taken from studies of actual practice. The guidelines will prove useless if they are *models for* continuing practice, in the sense of prescriptions of how educators ought to conduct themselves regardless of the specific context. If guidelines are to be used to judge practice, evaluated. Context is not an adjunct to understanding effective practice; rather, it is woven into the very fabric of practice.

Epistemological Basis of Practice: To fully explain effective practice, continuing educators must be able to describe how they do what they do. This description provides an understanding of the epistemological basis of their practice. The question that is of central concern here is: "What kind of knowledge or knowing characterizes effective practice? Another way to say this is: What does one need to know to be an effective practitioner? Schon has answered these questions by offering an epistemology of professional artistry.

An epistemology that can only offer an account of the declarative knowledge possessed by continuing educators is inadequate as a tool for understanding the complexity of practice. The program planning frameworks described in Chapter Seven are examples of declarative knowledge about continuing professional education. This type of epistemology does not adequately describe the forms of knowledge that distinguish the excellent educator from the merely adequate, or in Benner's terms, the expert from the notice. For example, many expert continuing educators cannot describe any one of the planning frameworks, whereas many novices can describe them in great detail. A more appropriate epistemology is needed to connect continuing educators' plans, techniques, ideals, and knowledge to the real judgments made in the unique, uncertain, and changing contexts of practice.

Schon responds to this need by suggesting that two forms of knowing are central to effective practice: knowing-in-action and reflection-in-action. In contrast to the epistemology that views practice as the application of knowledge, Schon assumes that continuing educators' knowing is in their actions. Many of their spontaneous actions do not stem from a rule or plan they were conscious of before their action. That is, continuing educators constantly make judgments for which they cannot state a rule or theory. In many cases this knowing-in-action does not solve a particular problem because the situations faced by continuing educators are unique, uncertain, or marked by conflicting values. Therefore, they need to construct the situation to make it solvable. The ability to do this, to reflect-in-action, is the core of effective practice.

Returning to our example, how did the university-based continuing educator decide whether or not to conduct a needs assessment for the continuing engineering education program? If Schon's analysis is correct, the continuing educator would make the best judgment under the circumstances if he were highly skilled at reflecting-in-action. What would this process look like? The assumption is that this is an indeterminate situation because it is not immediately obvious that a needs assessment should be conducted. The continuing educator's goal is to change this situation into a determinate one, one in which he is relatively certain about the correct course of action. Based on past experience, the educator has built up a repertoire of examples and understandings of situations like this. This repertoire of practical knowledge is used to make sense of the current situation, to see it as some prior situation in which his actions were successful. Once the current situation is framed in such a way as to make it solvable, the educator would probably conduct an on-the-spot experiment to test its appropriateness. This might be done during conversations with others, such as the training director or the head of the continuing education unit, to determine their satisfaction with the potential course of action.

If effective practice is not to be utterly context-dependent, its epistemology must account for a kind of knowing that can be used in most or all situations. Reflection-in-action is such an epistemology. Its use is a key to understanding effective practice in continuing professional education. This epistemology describes how continuing educators make decisions in areas such as developing and evaluating educative activities, fostering participation in such activities, and forming interrorganizational relationships. For instance, the entire program development process may be viewed as a form of reflection-in-action in which educators are continually framing ambiguous situations so as to make them solvable.

The interrelationship of the ethical, contextual, and epistemological bases of effective practice can be articulated as follows: *Effective practice in continuing professional education means making the best judgment in a specific context and for a specified ethical framework.* These judgments, which are made as a result of knowing-in-action and reflection-in-action, are evaluated as best against what is possible in the specific circumstances in which they occur and what is desirable within a particular ethical framework.

Improving practice

To improve practice, the abilities of continuing educators to make their "best judgments" must be facilitated. How can the ability to judge be facilitated by those who train continuing professional educators and by those educators themselves? To improve suggests a process of learning and thus, as discussed, this facilitation must be based on a model of continuing educators as learners. As with other professionals, it is essential to specify how they know and how they acquire this knowledge.

Continuing educators' knowing-in-action is acquired from their reflection-in-action undertaken in the indeterminate zones of practice and from the theory and research developed in continuing education and other fields. Reflection-in-action generates new knowledge by contributing new examples, understandings, and actions to educators' already existing repertoires. The acquisition of reflection-in-action appears to be less straight forward than the acquisition of knowing-in-action. Continuing educators reflect-in-action as matter of course in their everyday life and use these same processes in their practice. However, to improve this ability continuing educators must reflect on their reflection-in-action by describing what they have done. As they can more consciously describe how they reflect and what that teaches them, continuing educators can more readily employ that form of knowing in new situations.

Practice can also be improved by participating in formal educational programs. In formal educational settings, such as conferences, workshops, and graduate programs in continuing education, declarative knowledge about continuing professional education is most often stressed. To increase the likelihood that this knowledge will be incorporated into continuing educators' practice, it must be presented in such a way that continuing educators will use it to reflect on their own practice situations in the presence of the instructor. This type of process can build the educators' repertories of practical knowledge.

Experientially based methods, such as case studies, simulations, and role plays, are useful for developing this kind of knowledge. Practice can also be improved in these settings by helping continuing educators increase their ability to reflect-in-action. Schon's suggestive account of how this process can be coached, but not taught, is useful. Faculty in graduate programs and workshop presenters, for example, can assume the role of coaches by explaining how they would perform in given practice situations and by reflecting with participants on the ways in which they approach similar situations.

The primary responsibility for improving practice in work settings falls to continuing educators themselves. The major strategy is for continuing educators to see themselves as researchers of their own practice. Their goal should be to understand how they frame problems and their own roles, to uncover their own practical knowledge and the processes by which they use that knowledge. Individual reflections on practice can be fostered by institutionally supported activities, such as staff meetings where practitioners discuss how their practice is affected by the constraints of their organizational settings. A tremendous amount of practical knowledge generally exists in a collection of continuing educators at the workplace, which unfortunately is often not fully tapped by others. Supervisors often have a wealth of uncovered practical knowledge among their staff that is not systematically made available to everyone. Finding ways to identify and share this knowledge would offer many ways to improve the practice of individual educators, as well as the collective work of a given continuing education unit.

Continuing professional education researchers also have a role to play in improving practice. Their theoretical formulations and empirical studies have an important role in improving practice. However, much more effort and resources need to be expended in these efforts in order to improve practice. More research and development units need to be developed, such as the one at Pennsylvania State University, where a collection of researchers focuses on a particular area of continuing professional education. This could be done by any one of the four principal providers of continuing professional education or through the collaborative efforts of several providers. Some of their work should begin to focus on continuing educators' practical knowledge and the processes these practitioners use to make the best judgments, the effect of context on these judgments, and the ethical frameworks in which these judgments are made. Researchers can do this by examining their own practice as continuing educators or by working collaboratively with practitioners. Benner, Elbaz, and Schon have offered useful ways to conduct this type of research

Much of this book has focused on ways for individual continuing professional educators to understand and improve their own practice. However, this book is based on the premise that continuing educators in all the professions are working on similar educational processes and issues. Although the responsibility for improving practice must rest ultimately with individual continuing educators, the achievement of this goal can be facilitated by individuals who see themselves as part of the collective enterprise of continuing professional education.

13

Changing Patterns of Education

We are, currently on the threshold of changes as great as those that followed from Gutenberg's invention of the printing press in the middle of the fifteenth century and its introduction in England by Caxton. It was no accident that the last decades of that century saw the birth and development on the one hand of numerous educational institutions and on the other of humanistic studies in place of purely devotional ones. Such a cultural expansion could not have occurred if all books had had to be laboriously produced as manuscripts. In the sixteenth century the leaders of the Reformation, especially Calvin, promoted the idea of universal literacy, a concept which would have been unthinkable without the printing press. Yet this idea was in conflict with another great development of the same period, namely the evolution, primarily by Erasmus, of the concept of a liberal education. There was nothing democratic about Erasmus's concept; a liberal education was to be offered to the elite, the masses being required only to acquire skill in an occupation.

The liberal education of the minority that he advocated consisted mainly of classical literary studies leading to an intelligent comprehension of texts. Erasmus believed that such studies until the age of 18 were the sure foundation for any form of further study; that a man educated thus could subsequently learn any discipline.

We can still discern, in English society more than 400 years later, two schools of thought which reflect little more than the view of Erasmus on the one hand, and of Calvin on the other. We might even feel that, for all that has happened in that time, the overall patterns of education have changed very little. That is, of course, a gross exaggeration that yet contains a grain of truth.

What has happened is that we have—or very nearly have—achieved Calvin's goal of universal literacy through a system of compulsory schooling. Yet much of that schooling, given that the study of Latin and Greek has been largely abandoned, consists of the literary studies and the intelligent comprehension of texts that were advocated by Erasmus. This may well be wholly unsuitable for all *except* the elite. There is still a wide acceptance in practice of the idea that a liberal general education to the age of 16 or 18 is a fitting preparation for any career. Yet there has been, over four centuries, a steady acceleration in the rate of acquisition of new knowledge; and the complexity of each discipline has greatly increased. It seems to me that the pattern of education has not adjusted to this change so that we are now in a state of disequilibrium where there will have to be a massive quantal change in the educational pattern to restore the balance.

On the other hand there does not appear to be any sign that this disequilibrium is widely appreciated by the educational world; or, where it is appreciated, that there is any readiness to accept the massive changes that could restore the balance. There are, of course, many reasons for resistance to change. First, as Cornford said in *Microcosmographia Academica,* 'There is only one reason for doing anything; all the rest are reasons for doing nothing'. Most of us in education tend to think of the education that we received—which has, after all, fitted us for the important jobs we now hold!—as a reasonably good model for what we now do. This is a wholly understandable feeling and underlies many of our *laissez-fair* attitudes to education. Second, the current educational pattern has, over the years, led to the evolution of a whole range of service industries which depend upon a continuation of the system. One obvious one is the publishing industry—it is always said that a successful school book comes second only to the Bible as a money spinner. There are, therefore, even outside the teaching profession, a lot of vested interests in maintaining the current educational pattern.

Third, the profession too is concerned quite naturally about jobs and conditions of service and does not take kindly to the prospect of profound change.

Fourth, the politicians who growl about the inadequacies of the through-put of the educational system, blame the profession, the curriculum, the differences in the governance of schools, the lack of parental control, the indiscipline in schools—anything but the nature of the educational system itself, which only they can change. We spend nearly eight billion pounds a year on the system; but, for all the Acts that have been passed, we make only trivial alterations to it—tinkering at the edges.

So we see the overall situation as one where there exists a great disequilibrium on the one hand and a widespread reluctance to make changes on the other. These are not new phenomena. They have, I think, been there for many years. We have been poised on the brink of change. But recently the situation has been affected by a new factor—the communications explosion—which is liable to throw the whole situation into such a turmoil that the change actually comes about.

The communications explosion has led to a great increase in the demand for continuing education; and many new potential ways of offering education. Until the arrival of telegraphy and air transport the world was a very large one. News, even of events of cataclysmic importance, could take days, weeks, even months to become known. The advent of radio and more especially of television added drama to the immediacy of news. News of a disaster—famine, flood or pestilence—formerly arrived too late for any effective help to be made available. Thus the news might induce pity but did not induce concern. Nowadays we not only know of disaster as it happens, we are also presented with vivid pictures in full colour within a matter of hours. All over the world this new immediate and dramatic awareness of global events and problems has led to public concern. This, in turn, has led millions of people to realize that they lack the ability to participate in solving the problems since they possess neither the background knowledge to comprehend the nature of many global problems, nor the power to help solve them even if they had the knowledge.

I believe that this chain of awareness leading to concern leading to a demand for further education and for participation in governmental decision making is one clear result of the communications explosion. The education that adults come to demand because of this new factor is different from that which they needed because of the acceleration in the growth of new knowledge. The latter meant that updating and refresher courses became necessary for vocational needs. The new demand, stemming from concern, is only very partially satisfied for reasons that I shall explain later. I believe that there is real danger in our failure to meet demand, in that, if it is not satisfied, it may be suppressed by the incredible superficiality of the explanations offered by the mass media. Let me explain what I mean. Argument is rarely to be found on television. It is all too easy for one person to make an outrageous assertion. To counter that assertion by reasoned argument could take quite a long time—and that is never available. Thus an opponent can only fall back on a rapid but equally outrageous counter-assertion. There is never time for discussion of any issue in depth. Superficiality is the virtually invariable outcome. The seeker after understanding may thus come to the erroneous conclusion that there is no understanding, and the concern bred in him by his new awareness may, therefore, be suppressed.

The other effect of the communications explosion upon the educational pattern is, of course, better recognized, but as yet little applied. It is the wealth of technology that is already waiting to be brought to the service of education. Harold Wilson, in setting up the Open University, wanted the technology of mass communication to be harnessed to serve education. He was thinking primarily of television. Today television is only one of the powerful techniques available. Harold Wilson had been impressed by the use made of TV in the

USA for educational instruction in such programmes as *Sunrise Semester.*

I was myself less impressed when, a few years later, I studied what was being done. I found that there was a wealth of extremely sophisticated and versatile hardware—including systems of two-way TV link-up—which had cost millions of dollars to develop; but there was an accompanying dearth of software of any quality. No dollars had been spent on that! I saw some of the most sophisticated systems being used to show an inept lecturer writing simple algebra on a blackboard! The dollars were not being spent on the programmes; they tended to take a camera into a traditional classroom. One reason for this was that there was—and there still is—a belief that TV can be used as the main medium of instruction. I think that there is already good evidence that this is a fallacy. TV is a very expensive medium both in money and in the availability of air time. It is a compulsive medium, but I believe its message to be ephemeral—evanescent, if you like—unless it is almost immediately reinforced by reading. I am at odds with Mr. McLuhan—the medium is not the message. The most that can be claimed is that the message can be temporarily reinforced by the medium. I claim that in the Open University we use TV economically, sensibly and, to a considerable degree, effectively; but it is only twelve per cent of the teaching material.

TV was the technology envisaged by Harold Wilson in 1963; it is now only one of many communication technologies that can be used for education. It has for some years been possible to design systems of individualized self-paced instruction. Each pupil has access to a station in which is placed a complete set of instructional materials; text, tape, film loop, experimental equipment and so on. Following the instructions of a printed programme, he proceeds through each lesson in his own time and tests his own comprehension at intervals by a series of built-in self-assessment questions. Should he get stuck, he has, if the system is operating in an institutional setting, access to a tutor. This is actually very much the pattern used by the Open University but when teaching is home-based access to the tutor is necessarily much more limited. We have seen the same system in use at the sixty-formal level in an institution in Mexico where it revealed quite staggering differences in the rates at which pupils could progress. Surely there is a fairly simple lesson here: it is difficult *on academic grounds* to justify the principle of mixed ability classes in the face of such results. There may well be other justifications.

But this is still very simple technology. Nowadays one could provide at each station, for each pupil, a mini-computer and a television screen linked by modem to a telephone, thus providing two-way video communicator with a distant teacher, access to a national computer network, access on demand to the complete contents of a national library and access to film library. This could all be provided at home; there would be no real *academic* need for anyone to attend school or college or university. There are, of course, overwhelming non-academic reasons for continuing to have schools and colleges and universities; they are vitally necessary for all sorts of social reasons.

For the cost of one year's current expenditure on education a great deal could be done to establish such a new system. An investment of eight billion pounds is nevertheless a very large one and many people would demand pilot experiments to produce evidence that it would all be worthwhile, before agreeing to spend the money. But that would not work. There was only one way that the Open University could be started. It started big. There were no pilot experiments. In relative terms the investments was large; millions of pounds were spent before there were any students or any evidence that the university would work. It was, in my terms, a gigantic act of faith. In the view of the less charitable it was a gigantic gamble with public money, which just happened to come off. We consider that a new communications-based educational system can only be started if there is a further act of faith several orders of magnitude larger.

Modern neurophysiology has shown that the capacity of the human brain to develop synaptic connections between neurones is virtually infinite; but the number of connections actually made is decidedly limited. If one accepts that memory and the power of rational thought are in some way correlated to the number or quality of the networks of these synaptic connections then it follows that man has by no means yet reached the limit of his potential intellectual capacity. It is easy to jump unjustifiable from this conclusion to a further one, namely that because of this undeveloped capacity that is latent in everyone, all children are capable of far more intellectual achievement than they exhibit; and that the reason for their failure to achieve lies wholly in the environment. I do not propose to be drawn into the argument about whether such environmental factors are the *only* determinants of intelligence or whether there are genetic factors that are even more important determinants.

Suffice it to say that I am, myself, persuaded that both have a large part to play in determining the number and quality of the synaptic connections.

As educationists we can in any event, do nothing to modify genetic determinants; but we can, and should, do everything possible to try to make the environment of development approach the ideal. The problem of course is to determine what is that ideal environment. Most people would agree that, whatever it may be, it should be made available, as far as possible, to everyone. In other words we should aim not only at an ideal environment; we should also aim at equality of opportunity. Both are unachievable. One cannot compensate for the differences between parents in providing opportunities for their children unless one wholly eliminates the family unit; and even then one must replace it by the creche where the qualities of those adults chosen to look after the children will vary as greatly as do the qualities of parents. But the realization that equality of opportunity is unachievable does not remove our responsibility for trying to achieve it as far as is practicable.

There can be no better way of achieving equality of opportunity at school than by introducing the sort of individualized self-paced instructional system described above. It could provide *all* children in *all* schools with access to the *full* range of courses of study that were available nationally. These courses could be prepared by the best available experts. Materials of great sophistication and quality can be assembled at very high cost only if the number of pupils using them is also very high. Furthermore the range of courses offered in a national system could be very wide covering all sorts of subjects. Choices by pupils would be constrained only to the extent necessary to ensure an adequate breadth of experience; there would be plenty of opportunity for elective study.

All the available evidence points to the fact that children respond very positively to learning systems of this kind. I have the faith that makes me certain that nearly all of them would benefit in that they would be able to experiment with different subject areas until they found courses that excited and stimulated them. Furthermore, more than one teaching approach to the same subject area could be offered so that children could choose the most interesting approach for them. Their progress in such courses would, astonish the sceptics. In the experiment in Mexico one 16-year-old boy completed the Open University foundation course in mathematics in just three weeks, with full comprehension as determined by examination. He, of course, was very unusual.

We therefore believe very firmly that, given a national system of this kind, there would be two very significant outcomes. First the rate of progress through initial education would be speeded up very significantly for a large proportion of the pupils.

In the USA all children go to school at 6, half of them go on to college, a quarter graduate from college, and one in ten continues into post-graduate education. All this adds up to the fact that on average the US child will spend no less than sixteen years in full-time initial education, emerging to take his or her place in society only at 22 or more. This is the average. Some do not start work until they are middle aged. This seems to me to be an inordinately long time. In the eighteenth and nineteenth centuries it was not uncommon for some children to graduate from university between the ages of 16 and 18. I am sure that this could still be possible. In any case the rate of progress through initial education overall could be speeded up, and even a small shortening of the period would have very significant effects in reducing the total cost.

The second significant outcome, perhaps even more important, is that the system would make it very much more likely that more children would obtain the sort of education for which they were fitted and which they themselves wanted, so that their value to the nation would be greatly enhanced.

As I mentioned before, I am not advocating a home-based system of this kind. There are extremely important aspects of education that cannot be acquired in isolation. The whole area of socialization, of learning how to relate to other people, of coming to appreciate that others are more skilful than you, or have wholly different skills from your own—these are the areas that demand an institutional setting. A corollary to my new system would then be that these who supervise in schools would become very much less the specialist academics and very much more the group leaders, maintaining discipline, advising on sensible choices of courses, administering examinations, organizing games and external activities—being in fact guide, philosopher and friend to the pupils. I believe that this could be a very rewarding career; but of course many current teachers entered the profession with very different concepts of what their work would be. It would thus be surprising if such a dramatic change of activities were to be generally welcomed by the profession.

In summary, I think that a new system of initial education of this kind would improve the through-put and reduce the cost.

Let me turn next to the issue of continuing education which is also poised to disrupt the existing patterns of education.

For some years now people in many countries have come to realize that the pace of acquisition of new knowledge is not only very fast but is accelerating. All sorts of figures are quoted to dramatise the situation; as, for example, the calculation that more new information emerged last year than emerged in the whole of recorded history up to 1900. This sort of statement is easy to make and impossible to prove or disprove; but it indicates well enough the dilemma that we face. It follows that the traditional idea of Erasmus that the initial education that children are given can be a preparation—and an adequate preparation—for the whole of their working lives is simply no longer tenable. Much of what they learn at school, college and university will be out of date not just before they retire but even before they finish their initial education. It thus seems sensible to consider whether a period of initial education that *average* sixteen years is any longer sensible. Clearly education must continue throughout life to provide the updating and retraining that a modern career will demand.

In almost every developed country politicians have paid lip service to this need to continuing education, but in very few instances has anything significant been done to provide it. The main reason for this is, of course, that the costs of the initial education programme have escalated so much that the idea of adding to them the cost of a programme of continuing education especially if it made use of conventional techniques of teaching is unacceptable. The costs of initial education have escalated because of:

1. a growth in the number of children requiring schooling—the 'bulge' in the birth rate;
2. legislation increasing the period of compulsory schooling;

3. an increased voluntary tendency to stay at school for longer and go on to higher education;
4. an increase in the amount of information that is being taught. This follows from the accelerating pace of the acquisition of new knowledge: together with a failure to prune out of the curriculum the less necessary elements;
5. an increased complexity of provision, e.g., TV, science and technology, laboratory experience, language laboratories, sophistication of school music and drama and sport provision, etc;
6. an increased salary bill. Teachers were underpaid but had rewards of status in the community. The latter has been eroded and led to unionization and large salary demands.

The high cost of initial education which inhibits the development by the state of continuing education leads in turn to one of two conclusions. Either continuing education must be provided by a system that is not a charge on central government funds, by making individuals or employers meet the total costs; or the cost of initial education must be cut to make funds available for continuing education. The second solution has never been tried. In the UK we have so far followed the first of these courses. The result is that, although there is a great deal of continuing education of offer, the system is inchoate; there is multiple provision in some fields, and large gaps in others. Furthermore, the system is driven by the profit motive, in other worlds by the prospect of increasing income either for the individual or for the employer. It bears no necessary relationship to the needs of society or of the nation as a whole. This is the reason why it is difficult to meet the new demand for continual updating to which I referred earlier. It is not anyone's responsibility to pay for it.

If we could cut down the cost of initial education, how could we best provide an organized systematic programme of continuing education? This brings me to another major change in the pattern of education, namely the development of the concept of distance learning. Although there have long been commercially-based correspondence colleges, which mostly had rather poor records of academic success, it remained broadly true that, until the Open University came along, it was widely believed in academic circles that the only way to educate anyone was to arrange face-to-face encounters between him and a teacher, so that—and I quote—'two minds could rub against each other'.

This was a charming conceit for the elite of the nineteenth century; it is an intolerably expensive fallacy in the twentieth. It denies the possibility of mass education using the media. The Open University showed that people who wanted badly enough to be educated could in fact educate themselves, given high quality help through the mass media. The academic world has come to accept, as a matter of reason based on evidence, that this is so; but there is still a considerable emotional resistance to its full acceptance.

I have already hinted at the economies of scale that lie at the heart of any system of distance earning or indeed of any self-paced individualized instructional system.Teaching materials of quality are very expensive to produce. Consequently they must be used by large numbers of students before the cost per student becomes reasonable. It thus follows, quite inexorably, that the total cost must be large, because there must be lots of students. Everything about a distance learning system must, like everything in Texas, be big. This means that distance learning system must usually be government sponsored and may even then be beyond the reach of the governments of small countries.

On the other hand the system has much to commend it, especially when we come to consider programmes of continuing education. Let me list some of the reasons:

1. People can stay at work while studying, so that they suffer no loss of income and the country suffers no loss of productivity. No one need pay a maintenance grant.
2. Students can, if they wish, remain anonymous so that they run no danger of being stigmatized by their colleagues should they fail a course.
3. No capital expenditure on residential or teaching accommodation is required.
4. Scarce expert teachers can reach very large audiences.
5. Courses can be kept scrupulously up to date.
6. There can be nationally accepted qualification for successful completion of the course.
7. Given adequate numbers of students the running costs per student are low.

There are, of course, limits to what distance learning can do. It cannot provide the sort of apprenticeship training that is needed to acquire manual skills. But in those fields where it can be used, it offers almost the only cheap way of introducing continuing education on a large scale.

The growth of distance-learning systems in the last decade has therefore been very striking. There are now between twenty and thirty Open Universities in almost as many counties of the world, including, for instance, Pakistan, Israel, Thailand, Australia, Germany, Venezuela, the Ivory Coast, and Sri Lanka. They offer very different sorts of courses to their students, ranging from extremely simple tropical agriculture or health care, to recent developments in micro-electronics or computers. They also differ widely in the media used for distributing courses to the students, since the choice must depend upon the communication networks available in the country concerned.

This brings me to the last of the major changes in the patterns of education that I want to mention, namely the explosive developments that are occurring in the third world and in China.

Every developing country makes strenuous efforts to increase the literacy of its population, recognizing that this is an essential prerequisite for economic advancement; and it is characteristic that among the first priorities of each government is a teacher-training programme. The problems that many countries face are truly formidable. I remember being told by the Minister of Education from Delhi that his five-year plan called upon him to create more *new* places in primary schools than all the primary schools places in Britain. It was not only an immense task, it was also a very expensive one for a country with chronic economic difficulties.

Moreover the escalation in the cost of education in the developed countries, to which I have already alluded, makes the provision by the poorer developing countries of a system modelled exactly on the West so expensive as to be almost a pipe-dream. They must find a cheaper alternative. Yet they are, very properly, extremely suspicious of any system that has not already been tried and proved successful in the West. This is I think why there has been such an enormous interest in the Open University, which is a cheaper system, tried and proven in the UK, that offers the economies of scale which in a large developing country are of paramount importance.

I think that there is quite a good chance that it will be the developing countries of the third world, and perhaps in addition China—which is trying to counteract decades of neglect—that will first make the new patterns of education work. They will not have to surmount the barriers of vested interests and of professional pride that tend to inhibit change in the West, so they may well give the lead in introducing some of the changes in the patterns of education that I have tried to outline. This would indeed be a salutary lesson to us.

Index